Study Guide to Accompany

Food & Beverage Cost Control

6th Edition

Lea R. Dopson   David K. Hayes

Contributing Author Allisha Miller

Contents

To the Student   iv

Chapter 1   Managing Revenue and Expense   1

Chapter 2   Creating Sales Forecasts   17

Chapter 3   Purchasing and Receiving   32

Chapter 4   Managing Inventory and Production   57

Chapter 5   Monitoring Food and Beverage Product Costs   78

Chapter 6   Managing Food and Beverage Pricing   106

Chapter 7   Managing the Cost of Labor   127

Chapter 8   Controlling Other Expenses   157

Chapter 9   Analyzing Results Using the Income Statement   173

Chapter 10   Planning for Profit   199

Chapter 11   Maintaining and Improving the Revenue Control System   226

To the Student

All foodservice managers, regardless of the type of operation they are involved in, must understand and manage the costs associated with operating their business. *Food and Beverage Cost Control, Sixth Edition* focuses on helping you with the study of cost management to understand its logic and its systems.

The authors find the challenge of cost management to be creative, exciting, and fun! To be successful, talented foodservice managers must know where they want to take their operations and then apply their training and expertise to get there. As leaders of their cost control teams, managers must recognize that the quality of their leadership will be measured by the standards they set for themselves and for their operations.

This *Study Guide* is intended to provide you with the first step in what will be a lifelong and financially rewarding study of how to reach new heights in your management of food and beverage costs. The *Study Guide* is organized according to the 11 chapters in the text. Each chapter in this *Study Guide* provides the following helpful tools and learning aids:

- Learning Outcomes
- Study Notes
- Key Terms & Concepts Review
- Discussion Questions
- Quiz Yourself

The **Study Notes** are intended to help you better understand the content. The answers to **Key Terms & Concepts Review, Discussion Questions**, and **Quiz Yourself** are provided at the end of each chapter. All the information in this *Study Guide* can be used for reviewing the material and for testing your grasp of cost control concepts and techniques.

Special thanks go to Allisha Miller who assisted us with the creation of the *Study Guide*. We hope that this exposure to the study of cost management creates in you the same enjoyment that we have experienced in our careers. If so, the skills and tools you learn will ensure that your hospitality career will really take off, allowing you to go wherever you want to go and as far as your dreams will take you!

Good luck!

Lea R. Dopson
David K. Hayes

Chapter 1

Managing Revenue and Expense

Learning Outcomes

At the conclusion of this chapter, you will be able to:

- Apply the formula used to determine business profits.

    It is important that managers be able to calculate the amount of profit earned in their businesses. The ability to operate a profitable business is one of the major factors that determine managers' pay rates as well as the likelihood that they will be promoted to levels of higher responsibility in the organizations that employ them.

    For those who own their own businesses, it is imperative that they know the amount of profits their businesses generate.

- Express business expenses and profits as a percentage of revenue.

    While the expenses incurred and profits generated in a business can be expressed in a variety of ways, one of the most common ways to do so is as a percentage of revenue. As result, the ability to accurately calculate expense and profit percentages is a key skill that all good managers must acquire.

- Compare actual operating results with budgeted operating results.

    As you will learn in this chapter, a budget is a forecast of future operating performance. Managers compare their actual operating results with their budgeted operating results to identify areas where improvements in their businesses can be made. The ability to constantly improve their organizations is a key skill possessed by the very best managers in the hospitality industry.

Study Notes

1. Professional Foodservice Manager

- A professional foodservice manager is unique because all the functions of product sales, from item conceptualization to product delivery are in the hands of the same individual.

- Because foodservice operators are in the service sector of business, many aspects of management are more difficult for them than for their manufacturing or retailing management counterparts.

- A foodservice manager is one of the few types of managers who actually have contact with the ultimate consumer. The foodservice operator must serve as a food factory supervisor, as well as a cost control manager.

- Excellence in operation is measured in terms of producing and delivering quality products in a way that assures an appropriate operating profit for the owners.

2. Profit: The Reward for Service

- If management focuses on controlling costs more than on servicing guests, problems will certainly surface.

- Management's primary responsibility is to deliver a quality products and services to the guest, at a price mutually agreeable to both parties. You do not want to get yourself in the mind-set of reducing costs to the point where it is thought that "low" costs are good, and "high" costs are bad.

- When management attempts to reduce costs with no regard for the impact on the balance between managing costs and guest satisfaction, the business will surely suffer. Efforts to reduce costs that result in unsafe conditions for guests or employees are never wise.

- The question is whether costs are too high or too low, given management's view of the value it hopes to deliver to the guest and the goals of the foodservice operation's owners.

- The difference between what you have paid for the goods you sell and the price at which you sell them does not represent your actual profit.

- **Revenue** is the amount of dollars you take in.

- **Expenses** are the costs of the items required to operate the business.

- **Profit** is the amount of dollars that remain after all expenses have been paid.

$$\boxed{\text{Revenue} - \text{Expenses} = \text{Profit}}$$

- For the purposes of this book, the authors will use the following terms interchangeably: revenue and sales; expenses and costs.

- All foodservice operations, including nonprofit institutions, need revenue in excess of expenses if they are to thrive.

- Profit is the result of solid planning, sound management, and careful decision-making.

$$\boxed{\text{Revenue} - \text{Desired Profit} = \text{Ideal Expense}}$$

- **Ideal Expense** is defined as management's view of the correct or appropriate amount of expense necessary to generate a given quantity of revenue.

- **Desired profit** is defined as the profit that the owner wants to achieve on that predicted quantity of revenue. Profit is the reward for providing service.

- Revenue varies with both the number of guests frequenting your business and the amount of money spent by each guest.

- You can increase revenue by increasing the number of guests you serve, by increasing the amount each guest spends, or by a combination of both approaches.

- *Sustainable development* is a term used to describe a variety of earth-friendly practices and policies designed to meet the needs of the present population without compromising the ability of future generations to meet their own needs.

- The positive benefits that accrue when businesses incorporate green activities are significant and they are increasing.

- There are four major foodservice expense categories that you must learn to control.
    a. **Food costs** are the costs associated with actually producing the menu items. In most cases, food costs will make up the largest or second largest expense category you must learn to manage.
    b. **Beverage costs** are those related to the sale of alcoholic beverages. Costs of a nonalcoholic nature are considered an expense in the food cost category. Alcoholic beverages accounted for in the beverage cost category include beer, wine, and liquor. It may also include the costs

of ingredients necessary to produce these drinks, such as cherries, lemons, olives, limes, mixers like carbonated beverages and juices, and other items commonly used in the production and service of alcoholic beverages.

   c. **Labor costs** include the cost of all employees necessary to run the business, including taxes. In most operations, labor costs are second only to food costs in total dollars spent. Some operators find it helpful to include the cost of management in this category. Others prefer to place the cost of managers in the Other Expense category.

   d. **Other expenses** include all expenses that are neither food nor beverage nor labor.

3. Getting Started

- Good managers learn to understand, control, and manage their expenses. Numbers can be difficult to interpret due to inflation. Therefore, the industry uses percentage calculations.

- Percentages are the most common standard used for evaluating costs in the foodservice industry. As a manager in the foodservice industry you will be evaluated primarily on your ability to compute, analyze, and control these percent figures.

- **Percent** (%) means "out of each hundred."

- There are three (3) ways to write a percentage:

Common Form

In its common form, the "%" sign is used to express the percentage, as in 10%.

Fraction Form

In fraction form, the percent is expressed as the part, or a portion of 100, as in 10/100.

Decimal Form

The decimal form uses the decimal point (.) to express the percentage relationship, as in 0.10.

- To determine what percent one number is of another number, divide the number that is the part by the number that is the whole.

$$\frac{\text{Part}}{\text{Whole}} = \text{Percent}$$

- If we want to know what percentage of our revenue went to pay for our expenses, we would compute it as follows:

$$\frac{\text{Expense}}{\text{Revenue}} = \text{Expense \%}$$

- As long as expense is smaller than revenue, some profit will be generated. You can computer profit % using the following formula:

$$\frac{\text{Profit}}{\text{Revenue}} = \text{Profit \%}$$

- Modified profit formula:

Revenue – (Food and beverage costs + Labor costs + Other expenses) = Profit

- Put in another format, the equation looks as follows:

Revenue (100%)
- Food and beverage cost %
- Labor cost %
- Other expenses %
= Profit %

4. Understanding the Income (Profit and Loss) Statement

- An accounting tool that details revenue, expenses and profit, for a given period of time, is called the **income statement**, commonly referred to as a **profit and loss statement (P&L).** It lists revenue, food and beverage costs, labor costs, other expenses, and profit.

- The P&L is important because it indicates the efficiency and profitability of an operation.

- The primary purpose of preparing a P&L is to identify revenue, expenses, and profits for a specific time period.

- Common percentages used in a P&L statement:

1. $\dfrac{\text{Food and beverage costs}}{\text{Revenue}}$ = Food and beverage cost %

2. $\dfrac{\text{Labor costs}}{\text{Revenue}}$ = Labor cost %

3. $\dfrac{\text{Other expenses}}{\text{Revenue}}$ = Other expenses %

4. $\dfrac{\text{Total expenses}}{\text{Revenue}}$ = Total expenses %

5. $\dfrac{\text{Profit}}{\text{Revenue}}$ = Profit %

- The Uniform System of Accounts for Restaurants (USAR) is used to report financial results in most foodservice units. This system was created to ensure uniform reporting of financial results.

5. Understanding the Budget

- A **budget** is simply an estimate of projected revenue, expense, and profit.

- The budget is known as the **plan**, referring to the fact that the budget details the operation's estimated, or planned for, revenue and expense for a given period of time.

- All effective managers, whether in the commercial (for-profit) or nonprofit sector, use budgets.

- **Performance to budget** is the percentage of the budget actually used.

- The **28-day-period approach** to budgeting divides a year into 13 equal periods of 28 days each. This helps the manager compare performance from one period to the next without having to compensate for "extra" days in any one period.

- Percentages are used to compare actual expenses with the budgeted amount, using this formula:

$$\frac{\text{Actual}}{\text{Budget}} = \text{\% of Budget}$$

- If our budget is accurate, and we are within reasonable limits of our budget, we are said to be "in line" or "in compliance" with our budget. Use the concept of "significant" variation to determine whether a cost control problem exists.

- A significant variation is any variation in expected costs that management feels is an area of concern.

- If significant variations with planned results occur, management must:

    1. Identify the problem.
    2. Determine the cause.
    3. Take corrective action.

6. Technology Tools

- Most hospitality managers would agree that an accurate and timely income statement (P&L statement) is an invaluable aid to their management efforts. There are a variety of software programs on the market that can be used to develop this statement for you.

- Variations include programs that compare your actual results to budgeted figures or forecasts, to prior-month performance, or to prior-year performance. In addition, P&Ls can be produced for any time period, including months, quarters, or years. Most income statement programs will have a budgeting feature and the ability to maintain historical sales and cost records.

- As you examine (in this chapter and others) the cost control technology tools available to you, keep in mind that not all information should be accessible to all parties, and that security of your cost and customer information can be just as critical as accuracy.

Key Terms & Concepts Review

Match the key terms with their correct definitions.

1. Revenue _____

2. Expenses _____

3. Profit _____

4. Business dining _____

5. Ideal expense _____

6. Desired profit _____

7. Sustainable development _____

8. Food costs _____

9. Beverage costs _____

10. Labor costs _____

11. Other expenses _____

12. Percent _____

13. Statement of income and expense (income statement) _____

a. A period of time—that is, hour, day, week, or month—in which an operator wishes to analyze revenue and expenses.

b. A detailed listing of revenue and expenses for a given accounting period. Also referred to as a profit and loss (P&L) statement.

c. The dollar costs associated with actually producing the menu item(s) a guest selects.

d. The term used to indicate the dollars taken in by the business in a defined period of time (often referred to as sales).

e. Food is provided as a service to the company's employees either as a no-cost (to the employee) benefit or at a greatly reduced price.

f. The expenses of an operation that are neither food, nor beverage, nor labor.

g. Accounting method that divides a year into 13 equal periods of 28 days each.

h. The price paid to obtain the items required to operate the business (often referred to as costs).

i. The number "out of each hundred." Thus, 10 percent means 10 out of each 100. This is computed by dividing the part by the whole.

j. The profit that an owner seeks to achieve on a predicted quantity of revenue.

k. The percent of the budget actually spent on expenses.

l. The dollars that remain after all expenses have been paid (often referred to as net income).

m. A forecast or estimate of projected revenue, expense, and profit for a defined accounting period.

14. Profit and loss statement (P&L)	_____	n.	Management's view of the correct or appropriate amount of expense necessary to generate a given quantity of sales.
15. The Uniform System of Accounts	_____	o.	The costs related to the sale of alcoholic beverages.
16. Budget/plan	_____	p.	A detailed listing of revenue and expenses for a given accounting period. Also referred to as an income statement.
17. Accounting period	_____	q.	All expenses (costs), including payroll, required to maintain a workforce in a foodservice operation.
18. Performance to budget	_____	r.	Standardized sets of procedures used for categorizing revenue and expense in a defined industry, for example, *The Uniform System of Accounts for Restaurants (USAR)*.
19. 28-day-period (approach)		s.	Earth-friendly practices and policies that meet the needs of the present population without compromising the ability of future generations to meet their own needs.

Discussion Questions

1. List and determine (by indicating yes or no) the different tasks for which foodservice, manufacturing, and retailing managers are responsible.

Task	Foodservice Manager	Manufacturing Manager	Retail Manager

2. List and explain the three different forms of writing a percent.

_____

_____

_____

_____

3. List and describe the four major foodservice expense categories.

_____

_____

_____

_____

4. List the three things a foodservice manager should do when there is a significant variation between an operation's budget and its actual performance.

_____

_____

_____

_____

5. List two positive benefits that accrue when businesses incorporate green activities.

_____

_____

_____

_____

Quiz Yourself

Choose the letter of the best answer to the questions listed below.

1. When considering costs, foodservice managers must remember that low costs are good and high costs are not as good.
   a. True
   b. False

2. Revenue in the foodservice industry refers to the amount of money taken in by a business.
   a. True
   b. False

3. A cost, in the foodservice industry, is another term used to identify an expense.
   a. True
   b. False

4. Noncommercial foodservice institutions should only be interested in generating enough revenue to equal their operating costs.
   a. True
   b. False

5. Ideal expense is the correct amount of cost required to generate a specific amount of revenue.
   a. True
   b. False

Questions 6 through 9 are based on the following information:

A simplified partial annual P & L statement for The Limpopo River House is shown below:

Description	Dollars	Percentages
Revenue	$1,200,000	
Food & Beverage Costs	375,000	
Labor Costs	425,000	
Other Costs	100,000	
Total Expenses		
Profit		

6. What was the profit percentage for The Limpopo River House?
   a. 16.25%
   b. 25.00%
   c. 37.50%
   d. 63.50%

7. If the desired profit at this level of annual revenues was 18.0%, what was the operation's ideal amount of expense?
    a. $100,250
    b. $216,000
    c. $568,150
    d. $984,000

8. If the budget for food was $250,000 and the budget for beverages was $70,000, how much over budget was the operation in the food and beverage category?
    a. $45,000
    b. $50,000
    c. $55,000
    d. $60,000

9. What was the operation's labor cost percentage?
    a. 28.2%
    b. 30.4%
    c. 32.2%
    d. 35.4%

10. If total expenses in an operation were $425,000, and revenue was $465,000, what was the operation's total expense %?
    a. 91.4%
    b. 101.2%
    c. 111.4%
    d. 121.2%

11. Matt Dain is a foodservice manager. Last month his food expense equaled $60,000, his labor expense equaled $50,000, and his other expenses equaled $19,000. His revenue equaled $160,000. What was his total expense percentage?
    a. 80.6%
    b. 95.2%
    c. 115.6%
    d. 125.2%

12. What is the formula that managers use to calculate profit percentage?
    a. Revenues – Expenses = Profit %
    b. Expenses ÷ Profit = Profit %
    c. Revenue ÷ Sales = Profit %
    d. Profit ÷ Revenues = Profit %

13. What is the formula that managers use to calculate their food and beverage (F&B) cost percentages?
    a. Food and beverage expense ÷ Revenue = F&B cost %
    b. Food and beverage expense ÷ Total expenses = F&B cost %
    c. Total revenue – Food and beverage expense = F&B cost %
    d. Total expenses – Food and beverage expense = F&B cost %

14. What is the labor cost percent formula?
    a. Revenue % – Profit % = Labor cost %
    b. Labor expense ÷ Revenue = Labor cost %
    c. Revenue ÷ Labor expense = Labor cost %
    d. Number of employees – Revenue = Labor cost %

15. What is the formula that managers use to calculate other expenses percent?
    a. Other expenses ÷ Revenue = Other expenses %
    b. Other expenses ÷ Total expenses = Other expenses %
    c. Total revenue – Other expense = Other expenses %
    d. Total expenses – Other expenses = Other expenses %

16. Jackie Wong is a foodservice manager. Last month, his food expense equaled $95,000, his labor expense equaled $53,000, and his other expenses equaled $17,000. His revenue equaled $200,000. What is his profit percentage?
    a. 0.175%
    b. 1.75%
    c. 17.5%
    d. 175.0%

17. Ginger Lee is a foodservice manager. Last month her food expense equaled $70,000, her labor expense equaled $50,000, and her other expenses equaled $8,000. Her revenue equaled $160,000. What was her other expenses percentage?
    a. 0.5%
    b. 2.0%
    c. 5.0%
    d. 20.5%

18. What formula do managers use to calculate percent of budget?
    a. Revenue ÷ Budget = % of Budget
    b. Revenue ÷ Actual = % of Budget
    c. Actual ÷ Budget = % of Budget
    d. Budget ÷ Actual = % of Budget

19. Peggy Richards creates an annual budget for her food facility. Her annual utility costs budget is $75,000. What is the most Peggy can spend on utilities each month and still stay within her annual budget?
    a. $6.25
    b. $62.50
    c. $625.00
    d. $6,250.00

20. What will be the effect on an operation if its manager is able to increase the number of products each guest buys when visiting the operation?
    a. Revenue will go up and costs will go up.
    b. Revenue will go down and costs will go up.
    c. Revenue will go up and costs will go down.
    d. Revenue will go down and costs will go down.

21. Some managers use a budgeting approach that defines 13 equal operating periods, each of which consists of
    a. 27 days.
    b. 28 days.
    c. 29 days.
    d. 30 days.

22. If significant variations exist when comparing actual financial results to planned results, the first thing managers must do is
    a. modify the budget.
    b. determine the cause.
    c. identify the problem.
    d. take corrective action.

Chapter Answers to Key Terms & Concepts Review, Discussion Questions, and Quiz Yourself

Key Terms & Concepts Review

1. d	5. n	9. o	13. b	17. a
2. h	6. j	10. q	14. p	18. k
3. l	7. s	11. f	15. r	19. g
4. e	8. c	12. i	16. m	

Discussion Questions

1. List and determine (by indicating yes or no) the different tasks for which foodservice, manufacturing, and retailing managers are responsible.

Task	Foodservice Manager	Manufacturing Manager	Retail Manager
1. Secure raw materials	Yes	Yes	No
2. Manufacture product	Yes	Yes	No
3. Distribute to end user	Yes	No	Yes
4. Market to end user	Yes	No	Yes
5. Reconcile problems with end user	Yes	No	Yes

2. List and explain the three different forms of writing a percent.
    *   Common Form: In its common form, the "%" sign is used to express the percentage, as in 10%.
    *   Fraction Form: In fraction form, the percent is expressed as the part, or a portion of 100, as in 10/100.
    *   Decimal Form: The decimal form uses the decimal point (.) to express the percent relationship, as in 0.10.

3. List and describe the four major foodservice expense categories.
    *   **Food costs** include the expense of meats, dairy, fruits, vegetables, and other categories of food items produced by the foodservice operation.
    *   **Beverage costs** include alcoholic beverages of beer, wine, and liquor.
    *   **Labor costs** include the cost of all employees necessary to run the business, including taxes.
    *   **Other expenses** include all expenses that are neither food, nor beverage, nor labor. Examples include franchise fees, utilities, rent, linen, china, glassware, kitchen knives, and pots and pans.

4. List the three things a foodservice manager should do when there is a significant variation between an operation's budget and its actual performance.
   - Identify the problem.
   - Determine the cause.
   - Take corrective action.

5. List two positive benefits that accrue when businesses incorporate green activities.
   - Managers of green operations help protect the environment.
   - Increasing numbers of customers are committed to preserving the environment, and they most often seek to frequent and support businesses that are committed to this same goal.

Quiz Yourself

1. b	6. b	11. a	16. c	21. b
2. a	7. d	12. d	17. c	22. c
3. a	8. c	13. a	18. c	
4. b	9. d	14. b	19. d	
5. a	10. a	15. a	20. a	

Chapter 2

Creating Sales Forecasts

Learning Outcomes

At the conclusion of this chapter, you will be able to:

- Develop a procedure to record current sales.

  Foodservice managers must learn the methods used to keep accurate sales records. These records are essential for use in calculating their operating cost ratios such as food, labor, and other expenses percentages, as well as for help in accurately predicting future sales levels.

- Compute percentage increases or decreases in sales over time.

  In many cases, a foodservice operation's level of sales (revenue) will not remain constant. When managers do an excellent job of operating their facilities, sales frequently increase. When managers do not do an excellent job, or when other external factors such as the opening of a competitive business influences their operations, their sales may decline.

  Because sales can frequently increase or decrease over time, it is important that managers know how to calculate the relative size of those increases or decreases.

- Develop a procedure to predict future sales.

  Knowing an operation's estimated future sales is important so managers can schedule enough workers, and buy enough products, to properly service the guests they anticipate coming to their operations.

  When managers have an effective sales forecasting procedure in place, and utilize that procedure well, they can do a good job in estimating their operations future revenue in terms of number of customers to be served, the amount those customers will spend, or both.

Study Notes

1. Importance of Forecasting Sales

- The first question operating managers must ask themselves is very simple: "How many guests will I serve today?"—"This week?"—"This year?" The answer to questions such as these are critical, since these guests will provide the revenue from which the operator will pay basic operating expenses and create a profit.

- In an ongoing operation, it is often true that future sales estimates, or projected sales, will be heavily based on your sales history since what has happened in the past in your operation is usually the best predictor of what will happen in the future.

- A **sales forecast** predicts the number of guests you will serve and the revenues they will generate in a given future time period.

- You can determine your actual sales for a current time period by using a computerized system called a **point of sales (POS) system** that has been designed to provide specific sales information.

- Remember that a distinction is made in the hospitality industry between sales (revenue), and **sales volume**, which is the number of units sold.

- Sales may be a blend of cash and noncash transactions.

- With accurate sales records, a sales history can be developed for each foodservice outlet you operate and better decisions will be reached with regard to planning for each unit's operation.

2. Sales Histories

- **Sales history** is the systematic recording of all sales achieved during a predetermined time period. Sales histories can be created to record revenue, guests served, or both.

- **Sales to date** is the cumulative total of sales reported in the unit for a specific time period.

- A **reporting period** is the specific time period for which sales records are being maintained.

- An **average** or **mean** is defined as the value arrived at by adding the quantities in a series and dividing the sum of the quantities by the number of items in the series.

- The two major types of averages you are likely to encounter as a foodservice manager are as follows:

    1. **Fixed average** is an average in which you determine a specific time period— for example, the first 14 days of a given month. Then you compute the mean or average amount of sales or guest activity for that period.

    2. **Rolling average** is the average amount of sales or volume over a changing time period. Essentially, where a fixed average is computed using a specific or constant set of data, the rolling average is computed using data that will change.

- The use of the rolling average, while more complex and time consuming than that of a fixed average, can be extremely useful in recording data to help you make effective predictions about the sales levels you can expect in the future.

- **Guest count** is the term used in the hospitality industry to indicate the number of people you have served, and is recorded on a regular basis.

- When managers record both revenue *and* guest counts, information needed to compute **average sales per guest**, a term also known as **check average**, is provided.

$$\frac{\text{Total sales}}{\text{Number of guests served}} = \text{Average sales per guest}$$

- Most POS systems report the amount of revenue you have generated in a selected time period, the number of guests you have served, and the average sales per guest. Of course, the same data could be compiled manually.

- A **weighted average** is an average that weights the number of guests with how much they spend in a given time period.

- The weighted average sales per guest for two days is as follows:

$$\frac{\text{Day1 sales} + \text{Day2 sales}}{\text{Day1 guests} + \text{Day2 guests}} = \text{Two-day average sales per guest}$$

3. Maintaining Sales Histories

- A sales history should consist of revenue, number of guests served, and average sales per guest.

- Managers can also create sales histories about the number of guests served in a specific meal or time period (for example, breakfast, lunch, or dinner), or the method of meal delivery (e.g., drive-through sales vs. carry-out or dine-in sales).

- Managers should maintain sales history information that best suits their operations. That information should be updated at least daily, and a cumulative total for the appropriate time periods should also be maintained.

- In most cases, your sales histories should be kept for a period of at least two years. This allows you to have a good sense of what has happened to your business in the recent past.

- A manager of a new operation will not have the advantage of reviewing meaningful sales histories because they simply do not exist.

4. Sales Variances

- **Sales variances** are changes from previously experienced sales levels.

- The variance is determined by subtracting sales last year from sales this year.

$$\boxed{\textbf{Sales this year} - \textbf{Sales last year} = \textbf{Variance}}$$

- **Percentage variance** indicates the percentage (relative) change in sales from one time period to the next.

$$\frac{\text{Sales this year} - \text{Sales last year}}{\text{Sales last year}} = \text{Percentage variance}$$

or

$$\frac{\text{Variance}}{\text{Sales last year}} = \text{Percentage variance}$$

or

$$\frac{\text{Sales this year}}{\text{Sales last year}} - 1 = \text{Percentage variance}$$

5. Predicting Future Sales

- Depending on the type of facility you manage, you may be interested in predicting, or forecasting, future revenues, guest counts, or average sales per guest levels.

- Revenue forecast is calculated using the following formula:

> **Sales last year + (Sales last year × % Increase estimate) = Revenue forecast**

or

> **Sales last year × (1 + % Increase estimate) = Revenue forecast**

- Use the revenue increases you have experienced in the past to predict increases you may experience in the future.

- Using the same techniques employed in estimating increases in sales, the non-cash operator or any manager interested in guest counts can estimate increases or decreases in the number of guests served.

- The guest count forecast is determined by multiplying guest count last year by the % increase estimate, and then adding the guest count last year.

> **Guest count last year + (Guest count last year × % Increase estimate) = Guest count forecast**

or

> **Guest count last year × (1.00 + % Increase estimate) = Guest count forecast**

- Average sales per guest (check average) is simply the average amount of money each guest spends during a visit.

- Using data taken from the sales history, the following formula is employed:

> **Last year's average sales per guest**
> **+ Estimated increase in sales per guest**
> **= Sales per guest forecast**

- An average sales per guest forecast is obtained by dividing the revenue forecast by the guest count forecast.

$$\frac{\text{Revenue forecast}}{\text{Guest count forecast}} = \text{Average sales per guest forecast}$$

- It is important to note that sales histories, regardless of how well they have been developed and maintained, are not sufficient, used alone, to accurately predict future sales.

- Your knowledge of potential price changes, new or lost competitors, facility renovations, and improved selling programs are just a few of the many factors that you must consider when predicting future sales.

- Guest counts can be increased by undertaking green initiatives. It is important to market the products and services directly to the rapidly growing market segment of educated, savvy customers who care about the food they eat and their impact on the world around them.

- Implementing sustainable practices that focus on conservation as well as utilizing organic, seasonal, and locally grown products can help build customer and employee loyalty, as well as boost profits.

6. Technology Tools

- The importance of accurate sales histories for use in forecasting future sales is unquestionable. Your POS system can be invaluable in this effort. Many systems today can be utilized to do the following:

  1. Track sales by guest count
  2. Track sales by date
  3. Monitor cash vs. credit sales
  4. Maintain products-sold histories
  5. Maintain check average data
  6. Compare actual sales to prior-period sales
  7. Maintain rolling sales averages
  8. Forecast future sales in increments
  9. Maintain actual sales to forecasted sales variance reports
  10. Maintain reservations systems

- For those operations that rely on reservations to control bookings, software of this type is available to instantly identify repeat guests, giving the operator a display screen that can include such information as frequency of visit, purchase preferences, and total dollars spent in the operation.

- Reservations software makes it possible for operators to reward repeat guests by developing their own "frequent dining" programs, similar to a hotel or airlines' frequent-traveler programs.

- Restaurants can track customer complaints and, if desired, provide coupons to compensate guests for difficulties.

- Reservations-related programs such as these can store information on reservation demand, predict optimal reservation patterns, identify frequent no-show guests, and even allow guests to make their own reservations online.

Key Terms & Concepts Review

Match the key terms with their correct definitions.

1.	Sales forecast/projected sales	_____	a.	The process of reporting a time period for which records are being maintained. This may be of the same duration as an accounting period.
2.	Point-of-sale (POS) system	_____	b.	An average that combines data on the number of guests served and how much each has spent during a given financial accounting period.
3.	Sales volume	_____	c.	A prediction of the number of guests to be served and the revenues they will generate in a defined, future time period.
4.	Sales history	_____	d.	The average amount of sales or volume over a changing time period—for example, the last 10 days or the last 3 weeks.
5.	Sales to date	_____	e.	The number of units sold.
6.	Reporting period	_____	f.	The change in sales, expressed as a percentage, which results from comparing two operating periods.
7.	Average (mean)	_____	g.	The value arrived at by adding the quantities in a series and dividing the sum of the quantities by the number of items in the series.
8.	Fixed average	_____	h.	A record of sales achieved by an operator in a given sales outlet during a specifically identified time period.
9.	Rolling average	_____	i.	The mean amount of money spent per customer during a given financial accounting period (often referred to as check average).

23

10. Guest count _____	j.	An increase or decrease from previously experienced or predicted sales levels.
11. Average sales per guest _____	k.	A system for controlling hospitality operations' cash and product usage by using a computer processor and, depending on the size of the operation, additional computer hardware, communications devices and/or software.
12. Weighted average _____	l.	The cumulative sales figures reported during a given financial accounting period.
13. Sales variance _____	m.	The number of individuals served in a defined time period.
14. Percentage variance _____	n.	The average amount of sales or volume over a specific series or time period; for example, first month of the year or second week of the second month.

Discussion Questions

1. List and explain the two major types of averages a foodservice manager may encounter and what their formulas are to calculate them.

   _____

   _____

   _____

   _____

2. List three different types of information that may be used for maintaining sales histories.

   _____

   _____

   _____

   _____

3. Determine what three areas are involved in predicting future sales.

   _____

   _____

   _____

   _____

4. Determine five advantages that are involved with developing and using sales forecasts.

   _____

   _____

   _____

   _____

5. List two examples of green practices that can help build customer and employee loyalty, as well as boost profits of foodservice operations.

   _____

   _____

   _____

   _____

Quiz Yourself

Choose the letter of the best answer to the questions listed below.

1. In most cases, an operation's sales histories are a good predictor of its future sales.
   a. True
   b. False

2. A sales forecast predicts the number of guests to be served and how much they will spend.
   a. True
   b. False

3. An operation's sales (revenue) indicates the number of units sold in the operation.
   a. True
   b. False

4. A foodservice operation's total sales figure includes only its cash transactions.
   a. True
   b. False

5. In most cases, an operation's most accurate sales history would be constructed from records held in the operation's POS system.
   a. True
   b. False

6. An operation had sales of $1,200 on Sunday, $700 on Monday, $650 on Tuesday and $925 on Wednesday. What was the operation's Sales to Date for the four days?
   a. $ 2,475
   b. $ 3,475
   c. $ 4,475
   d. $ 5,475

7. Which piece of management information would include the most current sales data?
   a. fixed mean
   b. fixed average
   c. rolling average
   d. prior period average

8. To calculate an accurate check average, a manager must know the number of guest served in her operation and the
   a. number of hours the operation was open.
   b. amount of sales generated in the operation.
   c. number of employees used to serve the guests.
   d. amount of expense required to serve the guests.

9. What is an operation's average sales per guest if total sales are $156,200; number of guests served is 3,500; and its total expenses are $25,632?
   a. $ 22.07
   b. $ 44.63
   c. $ 66.07
   d. $ 88.63

10. An operation had sales of $1,000 and served 200 guests on Monday. On Tuesday, the operation served 150 guests and had sales of $900. What was the operation's weighted check average for the two days?
    a. $5.43
    b. $5.50
    c. $5.57
    d. $5.64

11. The best sales histories consist only of the number of guests served in the past.
    a. True
    b. False

12. The minimum time length for a good sales history is one full day of operation.
    a. True
    b. False

13. Sales histories are best updated on a daily basis.
    a. True
    b. False

14. Detailed sales histories should be kept for a period of at least five years.
    a. True
    b. False

15. Sales histories are of special value to managers of new foodservice operations.
    a. True
    b. False

16. A sales variance is determined by subtracting last year's sales from
    a. cost of sales.
    b. sales this year.
    c. forecasted sales.
    d. forecasted cost of sales.

17. An operation's percentage variance for revenue is equal to
    a. Variance – Sales this year
    b. Variance ÷ Sales this year
    c. 1 – (Sales this year ÷ Sales last year)
    d. (Sales this year – Sales last year) ÷ Sales last year

18. Last month an operation achieved sales of $67,263. This month the operation's sales were $69,872. What was the operation's sales variance for the month?
    a. $2,609
    b. $2,709
    c. $2,809
    d. $2,909

19. Last month an operation achieved sales of $68,263. The sales variance this month was $3,200. What was the operation's percentage variance in sales?
    a. 2.13%
    b. 4.69%
    c. 6.13%
    d. 8.69%

20. An operation had sales last year of $359,265 and sales this year of $245,968. What was this operation's sales variance this year?
    a. –$113,297
    b. –$2,987
    c. $2,987
    d. $113,297

21. A coffee shop forecasts it will achieve revenue of $102,500 next month, and that it will serve 25,000 guests. What is the operation's forecasted check average for next month?
    a. $2.44
    b. $3.10
    c. $4.10
    d. $6.44

    Answer: c
    Answer Note: $102,500 ÷ 25,000 = $4.10
    Difficulty: medium
    Section Reference: Predicting Future Sales
    Learning Objective: Develop a procedure to predict future sales

22. A manager forecasts a 5 percent increase in revenue for her operation next year. Which formula would she use to estimate the next year's revenue?
    a. Sales last year × 1.05
    b. Sales this year × 1.05
    c. Sales this year ÷ Sales last year
    d. Sales last year ÷ Sales this year

23. Which calculation will produce a manager's forecasted average sales per guest?
    a. Revenue forecast – Guest count forecast
    b. Revenue forecast ÷ Guest count forecast
    c. Guest count forecast × Revenue forecast
    d. Guest count forecast ÷ Revenue forecast

24. A manager served 30,000 guests last year and expects to serve 5 percent more guests next year. How many guests does the manager expect to serve next year?
    a. 28,500
    b. 30,750
    c. 31,500
    d. 33,750

25. Last year a manager's operation achieved $1,250,000 in revenue. The manager forecasts a 10 percent increase in revenue for next year. What is the manager's revenue forecast for next year?
    a. $1,100,000
    b. $1,375,000
    c. $1,650,000
    d. $1,925,000

26. An operation has an average sale per guest of $10.00. For the upcoming accounting period, the operation's manager predicts 5,000 guests will be served at a check average 5 percent higher than the current average. What should be this manager's revenue forecast for the upcoming period?
    a. $52,500
    b. $54,500
    c. $56,500
    d. $58,500

Chapter Answers to Key Terms & Concepts Review, Discussion Questions, and Quiz Yourself

Key Terms & Concepts Review

1. c	5. l	9. d	13. j
2. k	6. a	10. m	14. f
3. e	7. g	11. i	
4. h	8. n	12. b	

Discussion Questions

1. List and explain the two major types of averages a foodservice manager may encounter and what their formulas are to solve them.
   - Fixed average: The average amount of sales or volume over a specific series or time period; for example, first month of the year or second week of the second month. Formula: Total revenue/Number of days
   - Rolling average: The average amount of sales or volume over a changing time period, for example, the last 10 days or the last 3 weeks. Formula: Revenue of days/Number of days

2. List three different types of information that may be used for maintaining sales histories.
   - Revenue
   - Number of guests served
   - Average sales per guest
   - Particular menu item served
   - Number of guests served in a specific meal or time period
   - Method of meal delivery

3. Determine what three are involved in predicting future sales.
   - Future revenues
   - Guest counts
   - Average sales per guest levels

4. Determine five advantages that are involved with developing and using sales forecasts. (Choose any five of the following.)
    *   Accurate revenue estimates
    *   Improved ability to predict expenses
    *   Greater efficiency in scheduling needed workers
    *   Greater efficiency in scheduling menu item production schedules
    *   Better accuracy in purchasing the correct amount of food for immediate use
    *   Improved ability to maintain proper levels of nonperishable food inventories
    *   Improved budgeting ability

5. List two examples of green practices that can help build customer and employee loyalty, as well as boost profits of foodservice operations.
    *   Implementing sustainable practices that focus on conservation
    *   Utilizing organic, seasonal, and locally grown products

Quiz Yourself

1. a.	8. b.	15. b.	22. a.
2. a.	9. b.	16. b.	23. b.
3. b.	10. a.	17. d.	24. c.
4. b.	11. b.	18. a.	25. b.
5. a.	12. b.	19. b.	26. a.
6. b.	13. a.	20. a.	
7. c.	14. b.	21. c.	

Chapter 3

Purchasing and Receiving

Learning Outcomes

At the conclusion of this chapter, you will be able to:

- Use sales histories and standardized recipes to determine the amount of food products to buy in anticipation of forecasted sales.

    To properly maintain their costs, managers use historical sales records to estimate the number of guests they will serve in the future and what those guests will buy. After they make that forecast the menu items that will be chosen by guests can be predicted and the ingredients required to make those menu items can be ordered and maintained in inventory. Unless this process is carefully managed, an operation may not have the inventory items on hand needed to produce the proper number of consistently high-quality menu items sought by its guests.

- Purchase food and beverage products in a cost-effective manner.

    In many foodservice operations, there are literally hundreds of ingredients and items maintained in inventory. In operations that serve alcoholic beverages, there are additional inventory items that must be purchased and properly maintained in storage.

    Keeping track of the many ingredients required to produce an operation's food and beverage products can be challenging. As a result, foodservice managers must learn how to purchase their food and beverage products in a cost-effective and efficient manner.

- Implement proper procedures for receiving food and beverage products.

    "Receiving" is the term foodservice professional use when referring to the process of accepting delivery from their vendors of previously ordered items and ingredients.

    It is important to recognize that the quality of food and beverage products in an operation rarely increases when they are held in storage. In fact, the quality of products accepted during the receiving process represents the highest quality of those products the operation and its guests will likely experience.

Because this is true, all foodservice operations must implement proper procedures for receiving and caring for only those food and beverage products that consistently meet the quality standards of the operation.

Study Notes

1. Forecasting Food Sales

- The menu determines the success of most foodservice operations. Part of this success comes from being able to answer the questions, "How many people will I serve today?" and "What will they order?"

- As a good manager, what you want to do is prepare the "right" amount of each menu item you offer based on your estimate of the number of guest you will serve. The right amount would be the number of servings that minimizes your chances of running out of any items and also minimizing your chances of having excessive amounts of any items remaining for sale when you close for the day.

- Once you know the average number of people selecting a given menu item, and the total number of guests who made the selections, you can compute the **popularity index**, which is defined as the percentage of total guests choosing a given menu item from a list of alternatives.

$$\text{Popularity index} = \frac{\text{Total number of a specific menu item sold}}{\text{Total number of all menu items sold}}$$

- In most cases, if you know what menu items your future guests will select, then you are better prepared to make good decisions about the quantity of each item that should be made available to serve them.

- The basic formula for individual menu item forecasting, based on an item's individual sales history and resulting popularity index is:

$$\text{Number of guests expected} \times \text{Items popularity index}$$
$$= \text{Predicted number of that item to be sold}$$

- The **predicted number to be sold** is simply the quantity of a specific menu item likely to be sold given an estimate of the total number of guests expected.

- A variety of factors such as competition, weather, special events in your area, facility occupancy, your own promotions, your competitor's promotions, quality of service, and operational consistency come together to influence the number of guests you can expect to serve on any specific day.

- Sales histories track only the general trends of an operation. They are not able to estimate precisely the number of guests who may arrive on any given day. That is your job as a manager.

- Menu item forecasting helps predict what menu items guests will purchase when they arrive at your operation. Menu item forecasting is crucial if you are to effectively purchase needed food and beverage items.

2. Forecasting Beverage Sales

- Managers can forecast alcoholic beverage sales using the same popularity index and predicted number to be sold tools they use when forecasting the sale of food items.

- **Alcoholic beverages** are those products that are meant for consumption as a beverage and that contain a significant amount of alcohol. These products are generally classified as:

    Beer: Fermented beverages made from grain and flavored with hops
    Wine: Fermented beverages made from grapes, other berries and fruits.
    Spirits: Fermented beverages that are distilled to increase the alcohol content of the product; these are also referred to as **liquors**

- **Keg beer** is also known as **draft beer**, or beer in a form of packaging in which the beer is shipped in multigallon units for bulk sale.

- By reviewing data from a point of sales (POS) system, managers know exactly which beers, by brand and by packaging form, they have sold in the bar on a daily basis. This information can be used to estimate the number of specific beer products that will be ordered by their guests in the future.

- The ability to accurately forecast wine sales is important. In many operations the forecasting of wine sales must be divided into two parts:

    Forecasting bottled-wine sales
    Forecasting wine-by-the-glass sales

- Forecasting the sale of **house wines** refers to estimating the sales of modestly priced wines offered by the glass.

- The number of guests who order a **mixed drink** (a drink made with a spirit) can be recorded and analyzed. Unlike beer and wine sales information, however, estimating the exact drink guests will request can be difficult to determine because there are literally hundreds of different spirit drinks that can be made.

- As the amount of time and effort required to track specific drink sales increases, so does accuracy. Each manager must determine the level of control appropriate for his or her own operation. This is because there must be a relationship between the time, money, and effort required to maintain a control system and its cost effectiveness.

3. Importance of Standardized Recipes

- The **standardized recipe** controls both the quantity and quality of what the kitchen will produce. It details the procedures to be used in preparing and serving each of your menu items.

- Good standardized recipes contain the following information:

    1. Menu item name
    2. Total yield (number of portions produced)
    3. Portion size
    4. Ingredient list
    5. Preparation/method section
    6. Cooking time and temperature
    7. Special instructions, if necessary
    8. Recipe cost (optional)

- The following list contains arguments often used *against* standardized recipes:

    1. They take too long to use.
    2. My people don't need recipes; they know how we do things here.
    3. My chef refuses to reveal his or her secrets.
    4. They take too long to write up.
    5. We tried them but lost some, so we stopped using them.
    6. They are too hard to read, or many of my people cannot read English.

- Reasons *for* incorporating a system of standardized recipes include:

    1. Accurate purchasing is impossible without the existence and use of standardized recipes.
    2. Dietary concerns require some foodservice operators to know the exact ingredients and the correct amount of nutrients in each serving of a menu item.
    3. Accuracy in menu laws requires that foodservice operators be able to tell guests about the type and amount of ingredients in their recipes.

35

4. The responsible service of alcohol is impossible without adhering to appropriate portion sizes in standardized drink recipes.
5. Accurate recipe costing and menu pricing is impossible without standardized recipes.
6. Matching food used to cash sales is impossible to do without standardized recipes.
7. New employees can be trained faster and better with standardized recipes.
8. The computerization of a foodservice operation is impossible unless the elements of standardized recipes are in place; thus, the advantages of advanced technological tools available to the operation are restricted or even eliminated if standardized recipes are not used.

- Standardized recipes are the cornerstones of any serious effort to produce consistent, high-quality food products at an established cost.

- Any recipe can be standardized to produce a known number of servings (the recipe's yield).

- When adjusting recipes for desired yield (the total number of servings needed to be produced), two general methods may be employed:

  1. Factor method
  2. Percentage technique

- When using the factor method, you utilize the following formula to arrive at a recipe **conversion factor**:

$$\frac{\text{Yield desired}}{\text{Current yield}} = \text{Conversion factor}$$

- The percentage method deals with recipe weight, rather than with a conversion factor. It is sometimes more accurate than using a conversion factor alone. The proper conversion of weights and measures is important in recipe expansion or reduction.

- The percentage method of recipe conversion is as follows:

$$\frac{\text{Ingredient weight}}{\text{Total recipe weight}} = \% \text{ of total}$$

Then

$$\% \text{ of total} \times \text{Total amount required} = \text{New recipe amount}$$

- **Recipe Measure Equivalents:**

Volume Measures

US	Metric
1.05 quarts	1 liter
Gallon	3.79 liters
Quart	0.95 liters
Pint	473 milliliter
Cup	237 milliliters
Tablespoon (T)	14.8 milliliters
Teaspoon (t)	4.9 milliliters

Weight Measures

US	Metric
2.2 pounds	1 kilogram
1 pound	453.6 grams
¾ pound	340.2 grams
½ pound	226.8 grams
¼ pound	113.4 grams
1 ounce	28.4 grams

Note: 1 liter (L) = 1,000 milliliters (ml) and 1 kilogram (K) = 1,000 grams (g)

4. Purchasing Food

- Proper purchasing is essentially a matter of determining the following:
    1. What should be purchased?
    2. What is the best price to pay?
    3. How can a steady supply be ensured?

- **Auditors** are individuals responsible for reviewing and evaluating proper operational procedures. They can determine the potential for fraud or theft.

- If it is not possible to have more than one person involved in the buying process, the work of the purchasing agent/receiving clerk must be carefully monitored by management to prevent fraud.

- A **product specification** (spec) is a detailed description of a recipe ingredient or menu item. A spec is a way to communicate with a vendor so the vendor will deliver only the exact item you have requested.

- A properly prepared product specification will include the following information:

  - Product name or specification number
  - Pricing unit
  - Standard or grade
  - Weight range/size
  - Processing and/or packaging
  - Container size
  - Intended use
  - Other information such as product yield

- **Count** is a term used to designate product size. For example, 16- to 20-count shrimp refers to the fact that 16 to 20 individual shrimp of this size would be required to yield 1 pound.

- **Product yield** is the amount of product remaining after subtracting losses resulting from cleaning, trimming, cooking, and portioning.

- Knowing an item's product yield helps determine how much product must be purchased initially to have the desired product quantity needed after accounting for any product lost in an item's preparation.

- A **bid sheet** is used to solicit prices from alternative vendors.

- When buying products it is important to know that:

  - Suppliers have many prices, not just one.
  - Suppliers reward high-volume customers with lower prices.
  - Cherry pickers are serviced last.
  - Slow pay means high pay.

- Using one or perhaps two primary vendors tends to bring the average delivery size up and should result in lower per-item prices.

- Giving one vendor all of the operation's business can be dangerous and costly if the items to be purchased from that vendor vary widely in quality and price.

- **Ethics** is defined as the choices of proper conduct made by individuals in their relationships with others. Ethics come into play in purchasing foodservice products because of the tendency for some suppliers to seek an unfair advantage over their competition by providing "personal" favors to buyers.

- Using ethical behavior means asking:

  1. Is it legal?
  2. Does it hurt anyone?

3. Am I being honest?
4. Would I care if it happened to me?
5. Does it compromise my freedom as a buyer?
6. Would I publicize my action?

- A quick way to review the ethical merit of a situation is to consider whom you would tell about it. If you are comfortable telling your boss and your other suppliers about the considered course of action, it is likely ethical.

5. Purchasing Beverages

- Determining which wines to buy is a matter of selecting both the right product and packaging form. To do so, you must first determine if you will sell wine by the:

    - Glass
    - Split or half-bottle
    - Carafe
    - Bottle

- Common wine bottle sizes are:

Bottle Size (Capacity)	Common Name	Description
0.100 liters	Miniature (mini)	A single serving bottle
0.187 liters	Split	¼ a standard bottle
0.375 liters	Half-bottle	½ a standard bottle
0.750 liters	Bottle	A standard wine bottle
1.5 liters	Magnum	Two bottles in one
3.0 liters	Double Magnum	Four bottles in one

Note:
1 US quart = 0.946 liters
1 US gallon = 3.785 liters

- A **wine list** is a menu of wine offerings.

- **Vintner** refers to a wine's producer.

- Spirits are sold in a variety of bottle sizes.

Spirit Bottle Sizes and Capacities

Common Bottle Name	Metric Capacity	Fluid Ounce Capacity
Miniature	50 ml	1.7
Half-pint	200 ml	6.8
Pint	500 ml	16.9
Fifth	750 ml	25.4
Quart	1.0 L	33.8
Half-gallon	1.75 L	59.2

Note: 1 liter (L) equals 1,000 milliliters

- In the hospitality industry, the 750 ml and the 1-liter are the two most commonly purchased spirit bottle sizes.

- **Well liquors** are those spirits that are served when the guest does not specify a particular brand name when ordering, while **call liquors** (also called **premium liquors**) are those spirits that guests request by name.

- Beer is the most highly perishable of alcoholic beverage products and is most often packaged and sold with a **pull date,** or expiration date after which it should not be served. Beer typically is sold to foodservice operators in cans, bottles, or kegs.

6. Purchase Orders

- A **purchase order (PO)** is a detailed listing of products requested by a buyer. A PO may include a variety of product information but must always include the quantity ordered and the price quoted by the supplier.

- PO preparation can be simple or complex, but should always contain space for the following information:

    Purchase Order Information

    - Vendor information
    - Purchase order number
    - Date ordered
    - Delivery date
    - Name of person who placed order
    - Name of person who received order
    - Name of ordered item
    - Item specification #, if appropriate
    - Quantity ordered
    - Quoted price per unit
    - Extension price
    - Total price of order

- Delivery instructions
- Comments

- The advantages of a written purchase order are many and include:
    1. Written verification of quoted price
    2. Written verification of quantity ordered
    3. Written verification of the receipt of all goods ordered
    4. Written and special instructions to the receiving clerk, as needed
    5. Written verification of conformance to product specifications
    6. Written authorization to prepare vendor invoice for payment

7. Receiving Food and Beverage Products

- Proper receiving is a critical operational task. The requirements for effective receiving are:
    - Proper location
    - Proper tools and equipment
    - Proper delivery schedules
    - Proper staff training

- A **delivery invoice** is a seller's record of what is being delivered and the PO is the buyer's record of what was ordered.

- Some items should be standard in any receiving operation. These include:
    - Scales: Scales should be of two types: those accurate to the fraction of a pound (for large items) and those accurate to the fraction of an ounce (for smaller items and pre-portioned meats).
    - Wheeled equipment: Items such as hand trucks or carts should be available to move goods quickly and efficiently.
    - Box cutters: These are used to quickly remove excess packaging.
    - Calculators: Vendor calculations should be checked.
    - Thermometers: Food must be delivered at the proper storage temperatures.

- Products accepted for delivery must be at the proper temperatures:

Acceptable Temperature Range for Delivered Products

Item	°F	°C
Frozen foods	10°F or less	–12°C or less
Refrigerated foods	30° to 45°F	–1° to 7°C

41

- Receiving personnel should be trained to verify the following key characteristics of delivered items:

    - Weight
    - Quantity
    - Quality
    - Price

- **Shorting** is the term used to indicate that an ordered item has not been delivered as requested. **A credit memo** indicates an adjustment to a delivery invoice must be made due to shorting or some other reason. A credit memo requires the signature of the person delivering products and the person accepting the products.

- When receiving beverage products, the following items are of special concern and should be verified:

    - Correct brand
    - Correct bottle size
    - No broken bottles or bottle seals
    - Pull dates (beer)
    - Correct vintage or year produced (wine)
    - Correct unit price
    - Correct price extension
    - Correct invoice total

- When training staff to verify proper pricing, two major concerns should be addressed:

    - Matching PO unit price to delivery invoice unit price
    - Verifying price extensions and total

- **Extended price** is the unit price of a product multiplied by the number of units delivered. An extended price is calculated as:

    Unit Price × Number of Units Delivered = Extended Price

- Never assume extensions are correct because a computer did them!

- If a supplier consistently shorts your operation, that supplier is suspect both in terms of honesty and lack of concern for your operation's long-term success.

- Training your receiving clerk to assess and evaluate quality products is a continuous process.

- Some large operations use a receiving record when receiving food and beverage products. A receiving record generally contains the following information:

    - Name of supplier
    - Invoice number

- Item description
- Unit price
- Number of units delivered
- Total cost
- Storage area (unit distribution)
- Date of activity

8. Technology Tools

- This chapter focused on managing food-related costs by controlling the areas of standardized recipes, purchasing and receiving. There are a variety of software programs that are available that can assist in these areas, such as:

  1. Recipe Software can maintain and cost standardized recipes as well as maintain and supply dietary information by portion.
  2. Purchasing Software can compare bids, make purchase recommendations based on best cost/best value, and produce purchase orders based on established inventory levels.
  3. Receiving Software can prepare a daily receiving report and maintain receiving histories.

Key Terms & Concepts Review

Match the key terms with their correct definitions.

1. Popularity index   _____

2. Predicted number to be sold   _____

3. Alcoholic beverages   _____

4. Beer   _____

5. Wine   _____

6. Spirits   _____

7. Liquor   _____

8. Keg beer   _____

9. Draft beer   _____

10. House wines   _____

11. Mixed drink   _____

12. Standardized recipe   _____

13. Recipe-ready   _____

14. Conversion factor (recipe)   _____

a. A term commonly used to describe spirits.

b. A method of determining the number of a given menu item that is likely to be sold if the total number of customers to be served is known.

c. A detailed description of an ingredient or menu item.

d. The percentage of total guests choosing a given menu item from a list of menu alternatives.

e. The amount of product remaining after cooking, trimming, portioning, or cleaning.

f. Expensive call liquors.

g. A listing of products requested by the purchasing agent. This document lists various product information, including quantity ordered and price quoted by the vendor.

h. A fermented beverage made from grain and flavored with hops.

i. A menu of wine offerings.

j. Those spirits that are served by an operation when the customer does not specify a particular brand name.

k. Those hours of the day in which an operation will not accept food and beverage deliveries.

l. A customer who buys only those items from a supplier that are the lowest in price among the supplier's competition.

m. A fermented beverage made from grapes, fruits, or berries.

n. A listing of several vendors' bid prices on selected items that results in the selection of a vendor, based on the best price.

15. Product specification (spec)   _____   o.   A drink made with spirits.

16. Count   _____   p.   The procedures to be used for consistently preparing and serving a given menu item.

17. Product yield   _____   q.   An addendum to the vendor's delivery slip (invoice) that reconciles differences between the delivery slip and the purchase order.

18. Bid sheet   _____   r.   A number used in the process of adjusting recipe yield.

19. Price comparison sheet   _____   s.   Fermented beverages that are distilled to increase the alcohol content of the product.

20. Cherry pickers   _____   t.   A price mutually agreed upon by supplier and operator. This price is the amount to be paid for a product or products over a prescribed period of time.

21. Ethics   _____   u.   The price per unit multiplied by the number of units. This refers to a total unit price on a delivery slip or invoice.

22. Wine list   _____   v.   A term used to identify beer products sold in multi-gallon containers.

23. Vintner   _____   w.   A term used to designate size. Size as established by number of items per pound or number of items per container.

24. Shelf life   _____   x.   The term used to indicate the type of wine to be served in the event a specific brand name product is not requested by the guest.

25. Well liquor   _____   y.   The choices of proper conduct made by an individual in his or her relationships with others.

26. Call liquor	_____	z.	A term used to describe beer sold in kegs.
27. Premium liquor	_____	aa.	Those individuals responsible for reviewing and evaluating proper operational procedures.
28. Pull date (beer)	_____	bb.	A wine producer.
29. Purchase order (PO)	_____	cc.	A seller's record of what is being delivered to an operation.
30. Auditor	_____	dd.	The hours of the day in which an operation is willing to accept food and beverage deliveries.
31. Delivery invoice	_____	ee.	When the vendor is unable to deliver the quantity of item ordered for the appropriate delivery date.
32. Acceptance hours	_____	ff.	A recipe ingredient that is cleaned, trimmed, cooked, and generally completed, except for its addition to the recipe.
33. Refusal hours	_____	gg.	Expiration date on beverage products, usually beers, after which they should not be sold.
34. Shorting	_____	hh.	Those spirits that are requested (called for) by a particular brand name.
35. Credit memo	_____	ii.	The period of time an ingredient or menu item in storage maintains its freshness, flavor, and quality.

36. Contract price   _____

jj. A form used to compare prices among many vendors in order to select the best prices.

37. Extended price   _____

kk. Those products that are meant for consumption as a beverage and that contain a significant amount of ethyl alcohol. They are classified as beer, wine, or spirits.

Discussion Questions

1. What two pieces of information are needed to calculate a menu item's popularity index?

   _____
   _____
   _____
   _____

2. Determine what two methods can be used to adjust recipes for quantity.

   _____
   _____
   _____
   _____

3. When purchasing items, what questions must first be determined?

   _____
   _____
   _____
   _____

4. List and explain the four most important features of receiving inventory.

   _____
   _____
   _____
   _____

5. Explain how managers can determine if their purchasing behavior is ethical.

   _____
   _____
   _____
   _____

Quiz Yourself

Choose the letter of the best answer to the questions listed below.

1. Low prices determine the success of most foodservice operations.
   a. True
   b. False

2. The right number of food items to prepare each day should be based on a manager's estimate of the number of guests to be served that day.
   a. True
   b. False

3. In the foodservice industry, popularity index is defined as the percentage of total guests choosing a given menu item from a list of alternatives.
   a. True
   b. False

4. The predicted number of a menu item to be sold is calculated as:
   Predicted number sold = Number of guests expected ÷ Item popularity index
   a. True
   b. False

5. Sales histories give foodservice managers a precise indication of the number of guests they will serve on any given day.
   a. True
   b. False

Questions 6 and 7 are based on the following information:

Menu Item	Number Sold	Popularity Index	Forecast # Guests	Forecast Item Sold
Beer	145			
Wine	275			
Spirits	380			
Total			1,000	

6. What is the popularity index for beer?
   a. .181
   b. .344
   c. .475
   d. .651

49

7. What is the number of forecasted wine sales? (Round up answer to the nearest whole number.)
   a. 244
   b. 310
   c. 344
   d. 410

8. Beer is a fermented beverage made from grain, and it is primarily flavored with
   a. hops.
   b. fruits.
   c. spices.
   d. berries.

9. Which type of beverage is distilled to increase its alcohol content?
   a. Wine
   b. Beer
   c. Spirit
   d. Draft beer

10. A house wine is most often a wine that is
    a. expensive and sold by the glass.
    b. expensive and sold by the bottle.
    c. inexpensive and sold by the glass.
    d. inexpensive and sold by the bottle.

11. Which piece of information is NOT typically included in a standardized recipe?
    a. Portion size
    b. Selling price
    c. Ingredient list
    d. Cooking time

12. A conversion factor is used when managers adjust a recipe's
    a. cost.
    b. yield.
    c. portion size.
    d. cooking time.

13. Which formula is utilized by managers for computing a conversion factor?
    a. Yield desired ÷ Current yield
    b. Current yield ÷ Yield desired
    c. Ingredient weight ÷ Total recipe weight
    d. Total recipe weight ÷ Ingredient weight

14. A recipe yields 60 servings. A manager wants to make 90 servings. What is the conversion factor the manager will use to adjust the recipe?
    a. 1.25
    b. 1.50
    c. 1.75
    d. 2.00

15. .95 liters is approximately equal to what amount?
    a. 1 cup
    b. 1 pint
    c. 1 quart
    d. 1 gallon

16. 1 pound is approximately equal to how many grams?
    a. 254
    b. 354
    c. 454
    d. 554

17. Which of the following terms should managers use to indicate a detailed description of a recipe ingredient or a menu item?
    a. Bid sheet
    b. Purchase point
    c. Delivery invoice
    d. Product specification

18. If a manager buys 6 pounds of 15–20 count scallops, how many scallops has the manager purchased?
    a. 60–85
    b. 75–100
    c. 90–120
    d. 110–140

19. The amount of a product remaining after it is cleaned, trimmed, cooked and portioned is referred to as the product's
    a. bid.
    b. yield.
    c. factor.
    d. specification.

20. Which of the following tools do managers use to gather pricing information from their suppliers?
    a. Purchase Order
    b. bid sheet
    c. credit memo
    d. delivery invoice

21. One way for a manager to determine if a potential action is ethical is to ask if that manager would share information about it with his or her
    a. spouse.
    b. customers.
    c. supervisor.
    d. co-managers.

22. A standard wine bottle contains 1.5 liters.
    a. True
    b. False

23. A "split" is equal to ¼ of a standard wine bottle.
    a. True
    b. False

24. A well liquor is one that is served to a guest who does NOT call for a specific brand when ordering a drink.
    a. True
    b. False

25. Wine is the most perishable alcoholic beverage.
    a. True
    b. False

26. Pull dates are most often utilized for beer products.
    a. True
    b. False

27. Purchase orders (POs) are detailed listings of products prepared by an operation's vendors to ensure they offer the lowest possible prices.
    a. True
    b. False

28. Purchase orders should always contain detailed information about quantities ordered and prices to be paid.
    a. True
    b. False

29. One advantage of purchase orders is that they verify quoted prices.
    a. True
    b. False

30. It is necessary for all purchase orders to be numbered.
    a. True
    b. False

31. Purchase orders provide the written verification needed to pay an operation's vendors.
    a. True
    b. False

32. Who prepares an operation's delivery invoices?
    a. owners
    b. vendors
    c. managers
    d. receiving clerks

33. To do their jobs properly, what is the minimum number of scales for weighing that should be made available to receiving clerks?
    a. one
    b. two
    c. three
    d. four

34. What is the formula that managers use to calculate extended price on delivery invoices?
    a. Unit price + Number of items delivered
    b. Unit price × Number of items delivered
    c. Unit price ÷ Number of items delivered
    d. Number of items delivered – Unit price

35. An operation ordered and received 6 cases of corn. The extended price for the corn shown on the delivery index was $51.00. If the invoice was correct, what will the operation pay for each case of corn?
    a. $7.50
    b. $8.00
    c. $8.50
    d. $9.00

36. An operation ordered 85 pounds of prime rib at $6.25 per pound. 92 pounds were delivered. What should be the extended price shown on the delivery invoice?
    a. $531.25
    b. $550.00
    c. $561.25
    d. $575.00

37. What would be the acceptable temperature range for receiving refrigerated dairy products such as fresh milk or cheeses?
    a. 0° to 5°F (–17.8° to –15.0°C)
    b. 10° to 25°F (–12.2° to –3.9°C)
    c. 20° to 35°F (–6.7° to 1.7°C)
    d. 30° to 45°F (–1.1° to 7.2°C)

38. How many signatures are required when a credit memo is properly prepared?
    a. 0
    b. 1
    c. 2
    d. 3

Chapter Answers to Key Terms & Concepts Review, Discussion Questions, and Quiz Yourself

Key Terms & Concepts Review

1. d	11. o	21. y	31. cc
2. b	12. p	22. i	32. dd
3. kk	13. ff	23. bb	33. k
4. h	14. r	24. ii	34. ee
5. m	15. c	25. j	35. q
6. s	16. w	26. hh	36. t
7. a	17. e	27. f	37. u
8. v	18. n	28. gg	
9. z	19. jj	29. g	
10. x	20. l	30. aa	

Discussion Questions

1. Determine what two pieces of information are needed to calculate a menu item's popularity index.
   - Total number of a specific menu item sold in a defined time period
   - Total number of all menu item sold in the same defined time period

2. Determine what two methods can be used to adjust recipes for quantity.
   - Factor Method – Changes the number of portions in a recipe to the number of portions desired
   - Percentage Technique – Deals with recipe weight rather than conversions. This technique is sometimes more accurate.

3. When purchasing items what questions must first be determined?
   - What should be purchased?
   - What is the best price to pay?
   - How can a steady supply be assured?

4. List and explain the four most important features of receiving inventory.
   - Proper Location – The "back door" is usually where all the receiving is done. The receiving area must be adequate to handle the job of receiving, or product loss and inconsistency will result.
   - Proper Tools and Equipment – Some items are standard in any receiving operation, such as the following:
     - Scales
     - Wheeled equipment
     - Box cutter

- Thermometer
- Calculator
- Records area

- Proper Delivery Schedules – Scheduling should be during slow periods, were there would be plenty of time for a thorough checking of the products delivered.
- Proper Training - Receiving clerks should be properly trained to verify the following product characteristics:
  - Weight
  - Quantity
  - Quality
  - Price

5. Explain how managers can determine if their purchasing behavior is ethical.
Managers can determine if a proposed purchasing action is ethical by first asking:

1. Is it legal?
2. Does it hurt anyone?
3. Am I being honest?
4. Would I care if it happened to me?
5. Does it compromise my freedom as a buyer?
6. Would I publicize my action?

Quiz Yourself

1. b.	11. b.	21. c.	31. a.
2. a.	12. b.	22. b.	32. b.
3. a.	13. a.	23. a.	33. b.
4. b.	14. b.	24. a.	34. b.
5. b.	15. c.	25. b.	35. c.
6. a.	16. c.	26. a.	36. d.
7. c.	17. d.	27. b.	37. d.
8. a.	18. c.	28. a.	38. c.
9. c.	19. c.	29. a.	
10. c.	20. b.	30. a.	

Chapter 4

Managing Inventory and Production

Learning Outcomes

At the conclusion of this chapter, you will be able to:

- Implement an effective product storage and inventory system.

    To produce high-quality menu items, food and beverage managers must maintain their product inventories in a safe and cost-effective way. Most foodservice operations purchase and store a wide variety of perishable products. These products must be carefully maintained to ensure their continued high quality and to minimize their loss due to spoilage or theft.

    Effective product storage and inventory systems are important to all foodservice managers. Properly storing and maintaining records of products in inventory are essential skills that must be mastered by all foodservice professionals.

- Control the issuing of products from storage.

    "Issuing" is the term foodservice managers use to refer to the process of officially removing items from storage and placing them into production areas. If this process is not carefully maintained, product losses may reach unacceptable levels due to spoilage or theft.

    The proper control of the issuing system is also important for ensuring that managers obtain information they must have to purchase additional inventoried items as these items are needed.

- Manage the food and beverage production process.

    The actual preparation and service of an operation's menu items is one of the most important processes that can occur in a profitable foodservice business. Guest satisfaction is directly impacted by how well a foodservice operation prepares the menu items that it sells.

    Consistent, high-quality menu items are an important key to the continued success of any foodservice operation and, as a result, the production process used to create them must be carefully developed and managed.

Study Notes

1. Product Storage

- In most cases, after purchased items have been received, they must be immediately placed into storage. Food and beverage product quality rarely improves with increased storage time. In fact, the quality of most products you buy will be at its peak when the products you order are first delivered to you.

- **Inventory** refers to all of the stored food and beverage products in an operation. Inventory must be managed and controlled.

- Storage costs an operation money in terms of space and the fact that funds tied up in inventory items are unavailable for use elsewhere.

- After receiving staff have properly accepted the food products you have purchased, the next step in the control of food costs is that of properly storing those items. The storage process, in most foodservice establishments, consists of three main tasks:
    1. Placing products in storage
    2. Maintaining storage areas
    3. Maintaining product security

- When using the last in, first out, or **LIFO,** storage system, the storeroom manager intends to use the most recently delivered product (last in) before he or she uses any part of that same product previously on hand.

- In the case of some bread, pastry, fruit, and vegetable items, a storeroom clerk could be instructed to utilize the LIFO system because, for example, it makes little sense to sell stale pastries to guests when fresher ones are available in inventory.

- When using a first in, first out, or **FIFO,** storage system, you intend to rotate your stock in such a way that product already on hand is sold prior to the sale of more recently delivered product.

- When using the FIFO system, oldest products (first in) are used before newer products.

- FIFO is the preferred storage technique for many perishable and most all nonperishable inventory items.

- To maintain quality and security, delivered inventory items should immediately be placed into one of three areas:
    1. Dry storage

2. Refrigerated storage
3. Frozen storage

- Dry-storage areas should be maintained at a temperature ranging between 65°F and 75°F (18°C and 24°C).

- Shelving in dry-storage areas must be easily cleaned and sturdy enough to hold the weight of dry products.

- Slotted shelving in storage areas is preferred over solid shelving when storing food because slotted shelving allows for better air circulation around stored products.

- All shelving should be placed at least six inches above the ground to allow for proper cleaning beneath the shelving and to ensure proper ventilation.

- Dry-goods products should never be stored directly on the floor.

- Hallways leading to storage areas should always be kept cleared and free of excess storage materials and empty boxes.

- **Potentially hazardous foods** are those that must be carefully handled for time and temperature control to keep them safe.

- Refrigerator temperatures used to store potentially hazardous foods should be maintained at 41°F (5°C) or less.

- Walk-in refrigerators should have easily cleaned shelving units that are at least six inches off the floor and are slotted to allow for good air circulation.

- Freezer temperatures should be maintained at 0°F (–18°C) or less. Newly delivered products should be carefully checked with a thermometer when received to ensure that they are frozen and have been delivered at the proper temperature.

- Frozen inventory items should be carefully inspected to ensure that they have not been thawed and refrozen.

- Frozen-food holding units must be regularly maintained, a process that includes cleaning them inside and out on a regular basis and the constant monitoring of temperatures to detect possible improper operation.

- Beverage area security is crucial. A **two-key system** is often used to control access to beverage storage areas. The individual responsible for the beverage area has one key while the other key is kept in a sealed envelope in a secured area. In the event of emergency, the envelope can be opened.

- Beer in kegs should be stored at refrigeration temperatures of 36°F to 38°F (2°C to 3°C). Keg beer is unpasteurized and, thus, must be handled carefully to avoid spoilage.

- Pasteurized beer in either cans or bottles should be stored in a cool, dark room at 50°F to 70°F (10°C to 21°C) because it does not require refrigeration.

- Canned beer should be covered when stored to eliminate the chance of dust or dirt settling on the rims of the cans.

- Product rotation is critical if beer is to be served at its maximum freshness.

- The three components critical to managing wine storage are temperature, light, and cork condition management.

- Generally, wines should be stored at a **cellar** temperature of approximately 50°F to 57°F (12°C to 14°C).

- Heat is an enemy of effective wine storage.

- When storing wine, it should be exposed only to the minimum amount of light necessary.

- The cork protects wine from its greatest enemy, oxygen. **Oxidation** occurs when oxygen comes in contact with bottled wine; you can detect a wine that has been overly oxidized because it smells somewhat like vinegar. Oxidation deteriorates the quality of bottled wines.

- Bottled wine should always be stored in such a way (usually on its side) so that the cork remains in contact with the wine to stay moist.

- Proper wine storage procedures should keep the cork moist.

- Spirits should be stored between 70°F and 80°F (21°C to 27°C) in a locked or highly secure and dry storage area.

- Since spirit products have a very long shelf life and are not highly perishable they do not generally require refrigeration.

2. Inventory Control

- Proper inventory management seeks to provide appropriate **working stock**, which is the amount of an ingredient you anticipate using before purchasing that item again.

- **Safety stock** is the extra amount of an ingredient you decide to keep on hand to meet higher than anticipated demand.

- The actual amount of products you should keep in your inventory will vary based on a number of factors. These include:
    1. Storage capacity
    2. Item perishability
    3. Vendor delivery schedule
    4. Potential savings from increased purchase size
    5. Operating calendar
    6. Relative importance of stock outages
    7. Value of inventory dollars

- A **fiscal year** is 12 months (365 days) long but does not begin on January 1st.)

- Determining amounts in inventory for liquor products is most often more difficult than determining these same levels for food.

- Food items, as well as beers and wines can most often be counted for inventory purposes. Opened containers of spirits, however, must be valued also. The two basic methods used to do so are:
    1. Weight
    2. Visual estimate

- Proper inventory control requires that you monitor both the amount and value of items in inventory.

- Valuing, or establishing a dollar value for an inventory item, is performed using the following item inventory value formula:

    Item amount × Item value = Item inventory value

- Item value must be determined by using either the LIFO or the FIFO method. When the LIFO method is in use, the item's value is the price paid for the least recent (oldest) addition to item amount. If the FIFO method is in use, the item value is said to be the price paid for the most recent (newest) product on hand.

3. Product Issuing and Restocking

- **Issuing** is the process of removing needed beverage, food, and supply products from inventory.

- A **requisition** is a formal request to have products issued from storage.

- Food, beverages, and supplies should be requisitioned only as needed based on approved production schedules.

- Needed items should be issued only with management approval.

- If a written record of issues is to be kept, each person removing food, beverages, or supplies from the storage area must sign, acknowledging receipt of the products.

- Products that do not ultimately get used should be returned to the storage area, and their return should be recorded.

- The basic principles of product issuing that apply to food and supplies also apply to beverages.

- Although various systems could be used for issuing liquor, many managers favor the **empty for full system** of liquor replacement. In this system, each bartender is required to hold empty liquor bottles in the bar or a closely adjacent area.

- The issuing of wine from a wine cellar is a special case of product issuing because these sales cannot be predicted as accurately as sales of other alcoholic beverage products.

- Regardless of the methods used by employees to requisition food and beverage products or the systems management uses to issue these products, inventory levels in an operation will be reduced as sales are made.

- A **physical inventory** system is one in which an actual physical count and valuation of all inventory on hand is taken at the close of an accounting period.

- A **perpetual inventory** system is one in which the entire inventory is counted and recorded, and then additions to and deletions from total inventory are recorded as they occur.

- A **bin card** is simply an index card (or line on a spreadsheet) that details additions to and deletions from a given product's inventory level.

- Utilizing the best features of physical and perpetual inventory systems is exactly what the ABC inventory system was designed to do. It separates inventory items into three main categories:

- **Category A** items are those that require tight control and the most accurate record keeping. These are typically high-value items, and though few in numbers, they can make up 70 to 80 percent of the total inventory value.

- **Category B** items are those that make up 10 to 15 percent of the inventory value and require only routine control and record keeping.

- **Category C** items make up only 5 to 10 percent of the inventory value. These items require only the simplest of inventory control systems.

- The ABC system focuses management's attention on the essential few items in inventory, while focusing less attention on the many low-cost, slower-moving items.

- The ABC system can also be used to arrange storerooms or to determine which items should be stored in the most secure areas.

- A **purchase point** is the point at which an item should be reordered and its inventory level replenished. An item's purchase point can be identified by one of two methods:

    1. As needed (just-in-time)
    2. Par level

- To use the **as-needed**, or **just-in-time**, method of determining an item's purchase point, you are basically purchasing food based on your prediction of unit sales and the sum of the ingredients (from standardized recipes) necessary to produce those sales.

- The **par level** is the amount of an item that should be held in inventory at all times.

4. Managing Food Production

- Managing the food production process means controlling five key areas:
    1. Waste
    2. Overcooking
    3. Overportioning
    4. Improper carryover utilization
    5. Inappropriate make or buy decisions

- Portion cost is the amount it costs an operation to produce one serving of a menu item. Portion cost is one important factor in establishing the selling prices of menu items. For that reason and for many others, the ability to calculate a portion cost correctly is an important management skill.

- **Food scoops** are sized based on the number of servings per quart of product served. Thus, a #12 scoop will yield 12 servings per quart and a #20 scoop will yield 20 servings per quart.

- **Convenience foods** or **ready foods** are those that are pre-prepared in some fashion.

- A complete food production schedule process will require you to:
    1. Maintain sales histories.
    2. Forecast future sales levels.
    3. Purchase and store needed food and beverage supplies.
    4. Plan daily production schedules.
    5. Issue needed products to production areas.
    6. Manage the food and beverage production process.

5. Managing Beverage Production

- In its simplest, but also its least desired form, beverage production can consist simply of a bartender **free-pouring**, which is making a drink by pouring liquor from a bottle, but without carefully measuring the poured amount.

- A **jigger** is a device (like a small cup) used to measure alcoholic beverages, typically in ounces and fraction of ounce quantities.

- Pour spouts are inserted into bottles and are available to dispense a variety of different quantities. When using a metered pour spout the predetermined portion of product is dispensed whenever the bartender is called upon to serve that product.

- In some large operations, beverage guns are connected directly to liquor bottles of various sizes. The gun may be activated by pushing a mechanical or electronic button built into the gun or the POS.

- The most expensive and most complete beverage production control solution is a **total bar system.** Depending on the level of sophistication and cost the total bar system can perform one or all of the following tasks:

    1. Record beverage sale by brand.
    2. Record who made the sale.
    3. Record sales dollars and/or post the sale to a guest room folio (bill) in a hotel.
    4. Measure and dispense liquor for drinks.
    5. Add predetermined mixes to drink.
    6. Reduce liquor values from beverage inventory value totals as drink sales are made.
    7. Prepare liquor requisitions.
    8. Compute liquor cost by brand sold.
    9. Calculate gratuity on checks.

10. Identify payment method (e.g., cash, check, credit or debit card).
11. Record guest sales by table or check number.
12. Record date and time of sales

- In moderate doses, **ethyl alcohol**, the type of alcohol found in beverage products, acts as a mild tranquilizer. In excessive doses, however, it can become toxic, causing impaired judgment and, in some cases, even death.

- Most states have now enacted third-party liability legislation, which, under certain conditions, holds your business and, in some cases, you, personally responsible for the actions of your guests who consume excessive amounts of alcoholic beverages in your operation. This series of legislative acts are commonly called **dram shop laws.**

6. Technology Tools

- This chapter addresses concepts related to product storage, inventory management, issuing, and production. There are a variety of programs that assist managers in these areas. They include programs that:

    1. Maintain product inventory values by food category (i.e., produce, meat, dairy, etc.).
    2. Create "shopping lists" through production of daily inventory and comparison with production schedules.
    3. Report par stock levels, daily storeroom issues, and daily product usage.
    4. Maintain perpetual inventory.
    5. Compute LIFO or FIFO inventory values.
    6. Maintain inventory products database by vendor, storeroom location, product type, alpha order, etc.
    7. Report below-par inventory levels.
    8. Report daily cost of goods issued or sold.
    9. Interface with handheld bar code readers for accurate inventory count and price extension.
    10. Compute inventory loss rates.
    11. Develop production schedules based on weekly, daily, or monthly sales forecasts.
    12. Create product requisition (issues) lists based on forecasted sales.

Key Terms & Concepts Review

Match the key terms with their correct definitions.

1. Inventory   _____   a.   A form of deterioration in product quality resulting from poorly wrapped or excessively old items stored at freezing temperatures.

2. LIFO (last in, first out)   _____   b.   The range of temperatures (approximately 50°F to 57°F (12°C to 14°C) highly recommended for the long term storage of many types of bottled wines.

3. FIFO (first in, first out)   _____   c.   Additions to par stock, held as a hedge against the possibility of extra demand for a given product. This helps reduce the risk of being out of stock on a given item.

4. Potentially hazardous foods   _____   d.   A menu item or ingredient that has been purchased pre-prepared to reduce on-site labor cost or to enhance product consistency.

5. Freezer burn   _____   e.   The type of alcohol contained in intoxicating beverage products.

6. Two-key system   _____   f.   All of a foodservice operation's currently stored food and beverage products.

7. Recodable electronic locks   _____   g.   A bar device used to measure predetermined quantities of alcoholic beverages. It is usually marked in ounces and portions of an ounce.

8. Cellar temperature   _____   h.   An automated set of procedures that combine sales information with product dispensing information to create a complete beverage revenue and production control program.

9. Oxidation   _____   i.   A liquor inventory valuation system that requires the inventory taker to assign a product value based upon a visual inspection of a bottle's content. For example a value of 10/10 is assigned for a full bottle, 5/10 is assigned to a half bottle, and so on.

10. Working stock	_____	j.	A portion control device sized based on the number of servings per quart of product served.
11. Safety stock	_____	k.	The process of supplying food or beverage products from storage by management for use in an operation.
12. Fiscal year	_____	l.	Short for the word complimentary, which refers to the practice of management giving a product to a guest without a charge. This can be done for a special customer or as a way of making amends for an operational error.
13. Tenths system	_____	m.	An index card with both additions to and deletions from inventory of a given product. To facilitate its use, the card is usually affixed to the shelf that holds the given item. Used in a perpetual inventory system.
14. Inventory valuation sheet	_____	n.	The quantity of goods from inventory reasonably expected to be used between deliveries.
15. Physical inventory	_____	o.	Term used to describe a method of storage in which the operator intends to sell his or her most recently delivered product before selling the older product.
16. Issuing	_____	p.	The term used to describe a series of legislative acts that, under certain conditions, holds businesses and, in some cases, individuals, personally responsible for the actions of guests who consume excessive amounts of alcoholic beverages. These "laws" shift the liability for acts committed by an individual under the influence of alcohol from that individual to the server or operation that supplied the intoxicating beverage.
17. Requisition	_____	q.	The bartender is required to retain empty liquor bottles, and then each empty liquor bottle is replaced with a full one at the beginning of the next shift. The empty bottles are then either broken or disposed of, as local beverage law requires.

18. Ingredient room	_____	r.	A system to control access to storage areas.
19. Empty for full system	_____	s.	A menu item prepared for sale during a meal period but carried over for use in a different meal period.
20. Comp	_____	t.	The point in time when an item held in inventory reaches a level that indicates it should be reordered.
21. Perpetual inventory	_____	u.	When a food or beverage product is requested from storage by an employee for use in an operation.
22. Bin card	_____	v.	An inventory control system in which an actual or physical count and valuation of all inventory on hand is taken at the close of each accounting period.
23. Perpetual inventory card	_____	w.	A system of determining the purchase point by using management-established minimum and maximum allowable inventory levels for a given inventory item.
24. Purchase point	_____	x.	The kitchen production area of a foodservice establishment.
25. As needed (Just-in-time)	_____	y.	Start and stop dates for a 365-day accounting period. This period need not begin on January 1.
26. Par level	_____	z.	A process that occurs when oxygen comes in contact with bottled wine, resulting in a deterioration of the wine product.
27. Daily inventory sheet	_____	aa.	A locking system that allows management to issue multiple keys and to identify precisely the time an issued key was used to access the lock, as well as to whom that key was issued.
28. Back of the House	_____	bb.	A bin card that includes the product's price at the top of the card, allowing for continual tracking of the quantity of an item on hand and its price.

29. Portion cost	_____	cc.	A form that documents all inventory items, the quantity on hand, and the unit value of each item.
30. Food scoop	_____	dd.	Pouring liquor from a bottle without measuring the poured amount.
31. Carryover	_____	ee.	Foods that must be carefully handled for time and temperature control to keep them safe to consume.
32. Convenience foods (Ready foods)	_____	ff.	The product cost required to produce one serving of a menu item.
33. Free-pouring	_____	gg.	A form that lists the items in storage, the unit of purchase, and the par value. It also contains the following columns: on hand, special order, and order amount.
34. Jigger	_____	hh.	A system of determining the purchase point by using sales forecasts and standardized recipes to decide how much of an item to place in inventory.
35. Total bar system	_____	ii.	An inventory control system in which additions to and deletions from total inventory are recorded as they occur.
36. Ethyl alcohol	_____	jj.	A storeroom or section of a storeroom where ingredients are weighed and measured according to standardized recipes and then delivered to the appropriate kitchen production area.
37. Dram shop laws	_____	kk.	Term used to describe a method of storage in which the operator intends to sell his or her oldest product before selling the most recently delivered product.

Discussion Questions

1. List and explain the three types of storage areas.

   _____

   _____

   _____

   _____

2. List five of the seven factors that affect the amount of products managers should keep in inventory.

   _____

   _____

   _____

   _____

3. Explain the difference between physical inventory and perpetual inventory systems.

   _____

   _____

   _____

   _____

4. Identify and explain two special concerns that must be addressed when issuing alcoholic beverage products.

   _____

   _____

   _____

   _____

5. List and explain five areas that a manager must control in the food production process.

   _____

   _____

   _____

   _____

Quiz Yourself

Choose the letter of the best answer to the questions listed below.

1. Which product would best be stored using the FIFO system of inventory management?
   a. flour
   b. donuts
   c. croissants
   d. strawberries

2. For safe storage, all shelving should be
   a. made of wood.
   b. cleaned quarterly.
   c. at least six inches above the floor.
   d. able to hold a minimum of 400 pounds.

3. Potentially hazardous foods (PHFs) are those that must be carefully handled to control their temperature and
   c. age.
   d. cost.
   e. time.
   f. weight.

4. Keg beer must be kept refrigerated because it is
   a. expensive.
   b. carbonated.
   c. easily stolen.
   d. unpasteurized.

5. Cellar temperature for wine storage is approximately
   a. 0°F (–18°C) or less.
   b. 36°F to 38°F (2°C to 3°C).
   c. 50°F to 57°F (12°C to 14°C).
   d. 50°F to 70°F (10°C to 21°C).

6. Which beverage product is least perishable?
   a. wine
   b. beer
   c. soda
   d. spirits

7. A manager has 3.5 cases of beef base in stock. Each case cost $110.00. What is the inventory value of the manager's beef base?
   a. $330
   b. $385
   c. $440
   d. $495

8. A manager has 55 pounds of steak in inventory. The total item inventory value of the steak is $594.00. What is the per pound inventory value of the steak?
   a. $10.80
   b. $11.50
   c. $12.80
   d. $13.50

9. A manager values lamb leg at $4.50 per pound. The total value of the manager's lamb leg inventory is currently $346.50. How many pounds of lamb leg does the manager have in inventory?
   a. 72
   b. 77
   c. 82
   d. 87

10. When calculating accurate spirit inventory values, managers may choose to utilize visual estimates or to use product
    a. size.
    b. brand.
    c. weight.
    d. viscosity.

11. What is the formula that managers use to establish the item inventory value of their stored products?
    a. Item amount + Item value = Item inventory value
    b. Item amount – Item value = Item inventory value
    c. Item amount × Item value = Item inventory value
    d. Item amount ÷ Item value = Item inventory value

12. A "purchase order" is a formal request to have products issued from an operation's storage areas.
    a. True
    b. False

13. In an "empty for full" inventory issuing system, liquor bottles are immediately destroyed or discarded after the bottles' contents have been served to guests.
    a. True
    b. False

14. A physical inventory system is one in which an actual physical count and valuation of all inventory on hand is taken at the close of an accounting period.
    a. True
    b. False

15. A perpetual inventory system is one in which an actual physical count and valuation of all inventory on hand is taken at the beginning of an accounting period.
    a. True
    b. False

16. A bin card is most likely to be utilized in a perpetual inventory control system.
    a. True
    b. False

17. When using an ABC inventory system, Category A items typically make up 5 to 10 percent of an operation's total inventory value.
    a. True
    b. False

18. An inventory item's par level is the amount of that item that should be held in storage at all times.
    a. True
    b. False

19. A recipe makes 20 servings. The total cost of the food required to make the recipe is $10.80. What is the portion cost of each serving made using this recipe?
    a. $0.44
    b. $0.54
    c. $0.64
    d. $0.74

20. A recipe has a $2.15 portion cost. The recipe makes 40 servings. What is the total cost of food required to prepare this recipe?
    a. $84.00
    b. $85.00
    c. $86.00
    d. $87.00

21. A manager's operation uses a #12 scoop to portion cottage cheese. How many portions should the manager get from a one-gallon container of cottage cheese?
    a. 12
    b. 24
    c. 36
    d. 48

22. How many ounces are in a #20 scoop?
    a. 1.6
    b. 1.9
    c. 2.1
    d. 2.4

23. What is another term used to describe convenience foods?
    a. ready foods
    b. low-cost foods
    c. low-labor foods
    d. made-from-scratch foods

24. What is the first step that managers must take to effectively prepare a food production schedule?
    a. Issue products
    b. Maintain sales histories
    c. Forecast future product sales
    d. Purchase and store needed ingredients

25. It is difficult to control bar costs if bar employees
    a. free-pour.
    b. use jiggers.
    c. use pour spouts.
    d. refuse to free-pour.

26. What is the purpose of a jigger?
    a. Display spirits
    b. Measure liquids
    c. Record liquor sales
    d. Control garnish size

27. Which is the most expensive type of bar control system?
    a. POS
    b. total
    c. jigger
    d. free pour

28. Which is the common name for the type of alcohol contained in drinkable spirit products?
    a. ethyl
    b. propyl
    c. methyl
    d. isopropyl

29. Under dram shop laws, which individual can be held liable for acts committed by intoxicated persons?
    a. the person making the alcohol
    b. the person serving the alcohol
    c. the person drinking the alcohol
    d. the person delivering the alcohol

Chapter Answers to Key Terms & Concepts Review, Discussion Questions, and Quiz Yourself

Key Terms & Concepts Review

1. f	8. b	15. v	22. m	29. ff	36. e
2. o	9. z	16. k	23. bb	30. j	37. p
3. kk	10. n	17. u	24. t	31. s	
4. ee	11. c	18. jj	25. hh	32. d	
5. a	12. y	19. q	26. w	33. dd	
6. r	13. i	20. l	27. gg	34. g	
7. aa	14. cc	21. ii	28. x	35. h	

Discussion Questions

1. List and explain the three types of storage areas.

   - Dry storage: These areas should generally be maintained at a temperature ranging between 65°F and 75°F (18° to 24°C).
   - Refrigerated storage: These areas should generally be maintained between 32°F and 36°F (0° to 2°C).
   - Freezer storage: These areas should be maintained between 0°F and –10°F (–18° to –23°C).

2. List five of the seven factors that affect the amount of products managers should keep in inventory.

   1. Storage capacity
   2. Item perishability
   3. Vendor delivery schedule
   4. Potential savings from increased purchase size
   5. Operating calendar
   6. Relative importance of stock outages
   7. Value of inventory dollars

3. Explain the difference between physical inventory and perpetual inventory systems.

   - A physical inventory system is one in which an actual physical count and valuation of all inventory on hand is taken at the close of an accounting period.
   - A perpetual inventory system is one in which the entire inventory is counted and recorded, and then additions to and deletions from total inventory are recorded as they occur.

4. Identify and explain two special concerns that must be addressed when issuing alcoholic beverage products.

- Liquor storeroom issues: One method for liquor issuing is the empty for full system, which is replacing an empty bottle of liquor with a full bottle.
- Wine cellar issues: The issuing of wine from a wine cellar is a special case of product issuing because these sales cannot be predicted as accurately as sales of other alcoholic beverage products. If the wine storage area contains products valuable enough to remain locked, it is reasonable to assume that each bottled wine issued should be noted.

5. List and explain five areas that a manager must control in the food production process.

- Waste: Food losses through simple product waste can play a large role in overall excessive costs. Wastage can be as simple as not using a spatula to get all of the salad dressing out of a jar.
- Overcooking: It is a truism that prolonged cooking reduces product volume, whether the item cooked is roast beef or vegetable soup.
- Overserving: Overportioning on the part of service personnel has the effect of increasing operational costs and may cause the operation to mismatch its production schedule with anticipated demand.
- Improper carryover utilization: Food that has been prepared and remains unsold at the end of the operational day is called a carryover or leftover. If these carryover items are not handled properly or stored at the right temperature, the product will not have the same quality. Production schedules must note carryover items on a daily basis.
- Inappropriate make or buy decisions: Products that are already prepared are called convenience or ready foods, and can be of great value to an operation. These items do have a down side because they may cost more on a per-portion basis.

Quiz Yourself

1. a.	9. b.	17. b.	25. a.
2. c.	10. c.	18. a.	26. b.
3. c.	11. c.	19. b.	27. b.
4. d.	12. b.	20. c.	28. a.
5. c.	13. b.	21. d.	29. b.
6. d.	14. a.	22. a.	
7. b.	15. b.	23. a.	
8. a.	16. a.	24. b.	

Chapter 5

Monitoring Food and Beverage Product Costs

Learning Outcomes

At the conclusion of this chapter, you will be able to:

- Accurately calculate food and beverage costs and their cost percentages.

  In most foodservice operations the cost of food and beverages is the operation's largest or second-largest cost. Because that is true, it is vitally important that managers know how to calculate their food and beverage costs. In the foodservice industry these costs are most often reported as a total amount and as a percentage of revenue because, as revenue increases, product costs will increase as well.

  In many organizations, a foodservice manager's overall performance will be measured in large part by the manager's ability to control food and beverage costs and their related cost percentages.

- Compare product costs achieved in an operation against the product costs the operation planned to achieve.

  Effective foodservice managers plan their menus and establishing their menu prices based on their forecasted (budgeted) costs of producing and selling their menu items.

  When the actual costs of producing and selling products significantly exceed planned costs, corrective action must be taken. To best determine exactly where appropriate corrective actions should be taken, professional managers must know how to accurately compare the amount of product costs they actually achieve to the amount of product costs they had planned to achieve.

- Apply strategies designed to reduce an operation's cost of sales and its cost of sales percentage.

  All professional foodservice managers seek to maintain a proper ratio between product costs and revenue. In some situations, product costs must be reduced.

  When a manager is faced with the responsibility of reducing product costs, he or she can most often choose from a variety of options. Each option impacts the operation and its guest in different ways. As a result, it is important for managers to know the options available to them for reducing their product costs and their resulting operation's product cost percentages.

Study Notes

1. Cost of Sales

- An operation's food and beverage costs are typically reported two ways: (1) as a total dollar amount and (2) as a percentage of the operation's total sales.

- The *USAR* recommends reporting food cost separately from (alcoholic) beverage cost. When the amounts of an operation's individual food and beverage costs are combined, they are referred to as the operation's total **cost of sales.**

- The ability to accurately calculate and report an operation's cost of sales is an important management skill.

- In nearly all foodservice operations, a manager's ability to control cost of sales will be used as a primary measure of that manager's competence and his or her abilities.

- Managers should also know how to estimate, or forecast, their future product costs (cost of sales). When they can do that accurately, they are able to compare the cost of sales their operations' actually achieve to their cost of sales forecasts.

2. Computing Cost of Food Sold

- Managers use a very specific procedure to properly calculate their cost of sales and their cost of sales percentages.

- An operation's total **cost of food sold** is the dollar amount of all food actually sold, thrown away, wasted, or stolen. It is computed as follows:

Beginning Inventory
PLUS
Purchases = Food available for sale
LESS
Ending Inventory = Cost of food consumed
LESS
Employee Meals = Cost of food sold

- **Beginning inventory** is the dollar value of all food on hand at the beginning of the accounting period.

- **Purchases** are the sum cost of all food purchased during the accounting period.

- **Goods available for sale** is the sum of the beginning inventory and purchases.

- **Ending inventory** refers to the dollar value of all food on hand at the end of the accounting period.

- **Cost of food consumed** is the actual dollar value of all food used (consumed) by the operation.

- **Employee meal cost** is actually a labor-related, *not* food-related cost. Free or reduced-cost employee meals are a benefit much in the same manner as medical insurance or paid vacation. The cost of employee meals is subtracted from the cost of food consumed total and that amount is transferred to labor cost (see Chapter 7).

- It is important to note that ending inventory for one accounting period becomes the beginning inventory figure for the next period.

- The cost of food or beverage products may be transferred from one foodservice unit to another. For example, it is likely that fruits, juices, vegetables, and similar items are taken from the kitchen for use in the bar, while wine, sherry, and similar items may be taken from the bar for use in the kitchen.

- Transfers out of the kitchen are subtracted from the cost of food sold and transfers in to the kitchen are added to the cost of food sold.

- Calculating actual cost of food sold on a regular basis is important because it is not possible to improve your food cost control efforts unless you first know what your food costs actually are.

- In nearly all operations, cost of food sold is calculated on at least a monthly basis because it is reported on the operation's income statement (P&L). In many operations, these costs are calculated more frequently.

- To properly analyze an operation's cost of sales for a specific accounting period, managers must first determine the amount of food used in that period and the amount of sales achieved in the same period. When they have done so, they can calculate their **food cost percentage**.

- The formula used to compute an operation's food cost percentage is:

$$\frac{\text{Cost of food sold}}{\text{Food sales}} = \text{Food cost \%}$$

- Business owners and operations managers commonly establish targets for their food cost as well as for their other operating percentages.

3. Computing Cost of Beverage Sold

- To properly analyze an operation's **beverage cost percentage** for a specific accounting period managers must first determine the amount of beverages used in that period and the amount of beverage sales achieved in the same period. The formula used to compute an operation's beverage cost percentage is:

$$\frac{\text{Cost of beverage sold}}{\text{Beverage sales}} = \text{Beverage cost \%}$$

- The proper computation of a beverage cost percentage is identical to that of a food cost percentage with one important difference. Typically, there is no equivalent for employee meals because the consumption of alcoholic beverage products by employees who are working should be strictly prohibited. The cost of beverage sold formula is:

Formula for Cost of Beverage Sold

Beginning Inventory
PLUS
Purchases = Beverages available for sale
LESS
Ending Inventory = Cost of beverage sold

$$\frac{\text{Cost of beverage sold}}{\text{Beverage sales}} = \text{Beverage cost \%}$$

- The value of any transfers to and from one operating unit (e.g., kitchen, bar, or other defined sales unit) to another should be recorded on a product transfer form. The form typically includes a space for the amount of product transferred, the product's value, and the individuals authorizing the transfers.

4. Computing Costs with Transfers

- The value of transfers to and from one operating unit to another should be recorded on a product transfer form.

- After all appropriate transfers have been made, accurate cost of beverage sold and cost of food sold calculations can be made.

Cost of Food Sold with Transfers

Beginning Inventory
PLUS
Purchases
= Food available for sale
LESS
Ending Inventory
= Cost of food consumed
LESS
Food transfers from kitchen
PLUS
Beverage transfers to kitchen
Employee Meals
= Cost of food sold

Cost of Beverage Sold with Transfers

> Beginning beverage inventory
> PLUS
> Purchases
> = Beverages available for sale
> LESS
> Ending inventory
> = Cost of beverage consumed
> PLUS
> Food transfers from kitchen
> LESS
> Beverage transfers to kitchen
> **= Cost of beverage sold**

5. Utilizing the Cost of Sales Formula

- When managers use cost of sales formulas for food and beverages they are in a good position to perform three additional tasks that can improve the management of their operations:

  1. Calculating cost of sales for individual product categories
  2. Estimating daily cost of sales
  3. Comparing actual costs to attainable costs

- In some cases, managers want to know the proportion of total food cost accounted for by each product category. These categories, for example, could include meats, produce, and dairy products. You can compute your **category food cost %**, that is, a food cost percentage computed on a portion of total food or beverage usage by using a variation of the cost of food sold ÷ sales formula.

- The proportion of total cost percentages is calculated as:

$$\frac{\text{Cost in product category}}{\text{Total cost in all categories}} = \text{Proportion of total product cost}$$

- For example, the cost of meats proportion would be calculated as:

$$\frac{\text{Cost in meat category}}{\text{Total cost in all categories}} = \text{Proportion of total product cost}$$

83

- Managers can choose to calculate proportion costs for any category of food or beverage products they wish.

- Today's modern POS systems routinely report an operation's product sales by category and/or selling location. Because that is so, managers utilizing the same product categories when taking their beginning and ending inventories can calculate individual product category cost percentages as well as the overall cost percentages achieved in their operations.

- The best managers want to know their cost of sales on a daily or weekly basis, rather than only on a monthly basis. They could take a physical inventory every day and calculate an accurate cost of food sales. But taking an accurate physical inventory in most operations is a very time-consuming task.

- It would be convenient if you could have a close estimate of your food usage on a daily or weekly basis without the extra effort of a daily inventory count. Fortunately, just such an approximation technique is available.

- Use of the six-column form such as the one below allows managers to estimate their daily cost of sales.

Date: x-x-20xx thru x-x-20xx

Weekday	Today	To Date	Today	To Date	Today	To Date

- Utilization of the six-column form requires managers to use the following two formulas:

Six Column Food Cost % Estimate
1. $\dfrac{\text{Purchases today}}{\text{Sales today}} = \text{Cost \% today}$
2. $\dfrac{\text{Purchases to date}}{\text{Sales to date}} = \text{Cost \% to date}$

- In order for the six-column food cost to be an accurate estimate, you must make one important assumption: *For any time period you are evaluating, the beginning inventory and ending inventory amounts are the same.*

- In other words, over any given time period, you will have approximately the same amount of food on hand at all times. If this assumption is correct, the six-column food cost estimate is, in fact, a good indicator of an operation's food usage. (To see why, return to the cost of food sold formula presented earlier in this chapter of the study guide and enter exactly the same number in the beginning inventory and ending inventory portions of the formula. What did you discover?)

- The six-column form for estimating product usage has the following advantages:
  - It is very simple to compute, requiring 10 minutes or less of data entry per day for most operations (the cells in a six-column excel spreadsheet can be formulated to do the math for you).
  - It records both sales history and purchasing patterns.
  - It identifies problems before the end of the monthly accounting period.
  - By the ninth or tenth day, the degree of accuracy in the To Date column is very high.
  - It is a daily reminder to both management and employees that there is a very definite relationship between sales and expenses.

- Good managers want to be able to compare their actual product cost with the product costs that should be attainable in their operations.

- To determine attainable (ideal) product cost needed for producing their menu items, managers use **standardized recipe cost sheets.** A standardized recipe cost sheet is a record of the ingredient costs required to produce a standardized recipe.

- Managers use standardized recipe cost sheets to calculate their total recipe costs and their individual portion costs. Total recipe cost divided by the number of portions made (recipe yield) = portion cost.

- Standardized recipe cost sheets can be produced using any basic spreadsheet software. In addition to total recipe cost, information that may be included on a standardized recipe cost sheet includes recipe identification number, recipe type (i.e. salad, bread, and the like), number of portions produced, actual portion cost, previous portion cost, date and previous date the recipe was costed.

- To cost recipes, managers must know weight and measure equivalents and can sizes:

Weight and Measure Equivalents

Item	Equivalent
60 drops	1 teaspoon
3 teaspoons	1 tablespoon
2 tablespoons	1 liquid ounce
4 tablespoons	¼ cup
16 tablespoons	1 cup
2 cups	1 pint
2 pints	1 quart
4 quarts	1 gallon
4 pecks	1 bushel
16 ounces	1 pound

Common Can Sizes

Can Size	Quantity
No. 303	1¼ cups
No. 2	2½ cups
No. 2½	3½ cups
No. 5	7⅓ cups
No. 10	13 cups

- Most foodservice products are delivered to an operation in their **as purchased (AP)** state. This refers to the weight or count of a product as it is delivered to the foodservice operator.

- **EP** or **edible portion** refers to the weight of a product after it has been cleaned, trimmed, cooked, and portioned.

- AP refers to food products as the operator receives them, and EP refers to food products as the recipe or guest receives them.

- A **yield test** is a procedure used for computing your actual EP costs on a product that will experience weight or volume loss in preparation.

- The formula used to calculate product yields is:

Product as purchased (AP) – Losses due to preparation = Product edible portion (EP)

- For meats and seafoods, managers conduct a **butcher's yield test** that considers loss due to trimming inedible fat and bones, as well as losses due to cooking or slicing when they calculate their EP costs.

- When performing yield tests managers are interested in a product's waste percentage and yield percentage. **Waste percentage** is the percentage of product lost due to cooking, trimming, portioning, or cleaning.

- The formula used to calculate waste percentage is:

$$\frac{\text{Product loss}}{\text{AP weight}} = \text{Waste \%}$$

- Once waste percentage has been determined, it is possible to compute the yield percentage.

- **Yield percentage** is the percentage of product you will have remaining after cooking, trimming, portioning, or cleaning.

$$\text{Yield \%} = 1.00 - \text{Waste \%}$$

- If we know the yield % we can compute the AP weight needed to yield the appropriate EP weight required for a recipe by using the following formula:

$$\frac{\text{EP required}}{\text{Product yield \%}} = \text{AP required}$$

- To check your figures to see if you should use a particular yield % when purchasing an item, you can proceed as follows:

$$\text{EP required} = \text{AP required} \times \text{Yield \%}$$

- Good vendors are an excellent source for providing tabled information related to trim and loss rates for standard products they carry.

- Another way to determine product yield % is to compute it directly using the following formula:

$$\frac{EP\ weight}{AP\ weight} = \text{Product yield \%}$$

- Managers can only calculate recipe costs accurately if they know their edible portion costs. **Edible portion cost (EP cost)** is the portion cost of the item after cooking, trimming, portioning, or cleaning. The EP cost is useful to know because it represents the true cost of an ingredient or menu item based on its product yield.

- To compute actual EP cost per pound (or unit), managers use the following formula:

$$\frac{AP\ price/lb.}{Product\ yield\ \%} = \text{EP cost/lb.}$$

- Waste % and yield % can be known if records are kept on meat cookery, the cleaning and processing of vegetables and fruits, and the unavoidable losses that can occur in some products during portioning.

- If you are to draw reasonable conclusions regarding operational efficiency, you must be able to compare how well you are doing with how well you should be doing. This process begins with determining **attainable product cost,** the cost of goods sold figure that should be achievable given the product sales in a particular operation if avoidable losses were completely eliminated.

- When actual product cost and attainable product costs are known, you can compute a business's operational efficiency ratio using the following formula:

$$\frac{Actual\ product\ cost}{Attainable\ product\ cost} = \text{Operational efficiency ratio}$$

- Attainable product cost excludes any losses due to human error, such as overcooking, overportioning, waste, theft, and the like. Therefore, the attainable food cost is rarely achieved.

- In general, operational efficiency ratings in the range of 100 to 110 percent are attainable. Variance beyond that, however, can indicate serious product control problems. Ratios that are too high, that is, ratios above 110 percent, could be an indication of excessive waste, ingredient theft, spoilage, over portioning, or inaccurate recipe cost sheet computation.

- Operating efficiency ratings that are too low, that is, ratings in the 80 to 90 percent range, must also be avoided. Efficiency ratios such as these could be the result of miscalculation of the number of items sold, inaccurate ingredient costing, underportioning, incorrect standardized cost sheets, or errors in valuing inventory.

- When comparing their actual product costs with their attainable product costs managers use the following formula:

$$\frac{\text{Actual product cost} - \text{Attainable product cost}}{\text{Attainable product cost}} = \text{Cost percentage variance}$$

- While it is not possible to determine one range of variance acceptability that is appropriate for all food facilities, it is important for you to establish acceptability ranges for your own facility.

6. Reducing the Cost of Sales Percentage

- Most kitchen-related theft deals with the removal of products from the premises, since few kitchen production workers also handle cash.
- The following product security tips are helpful when designing control systems to ensure the safety and security of food (and beverage) products.

Product Security Tips
1. Keep all storage areas locked and secure.
2. Issue food only with proper authorization and management approval.
3. Monitor the use of all carryovers.
4. Do not allow food to be prepared unless a guest check or written request precedes the preparation.
5. Maintain an active inventory management system.
6. Ensure that all food received is signed for by the appropriate receiving clerk.
7. Do not pay suppliers for food products without an appropriate and signed invoice.
8. Do not use "petty cash" to pay for food items unless a receipt and the product can be produced.
9. Conduct systematic physical inventories of all level A, B, and C products.
10. Do not allow employees to remove food from the premises without management's specific approval.

- Employee product theft can occur in either the bar or the kitchen production areas, but it is often more prevalent in the bar areas.

- Bartender does not record a sale in the POS system, pocketing the payment from the sale.

- When bartenders overpour, they are stealing from the operation. When they underpour, they are shortchanging the guest.

- Often called "watering down the drinks," dilution of product is a method of bar or storeroom theft that involves adding water to the product to make up for spirits that have either been stolen or given away.

- When a specific call brand liquor has been ordered and paid for by a guest, it should, of course, be served to that guest. If, however, a bartender substitutes a less expensive well liquor for the call brand, while charging the guest for the higher priced call liquor, the bartender may intend to keep the difference in the prices paid for the two items. This has the effect of shortchanging guests, who paid higher prices for premium liquor drinks they did not receive.

- Some managers enlist the aid of a **spotter**, a professional who, for a fee, will observe the bar operation. Commonly known as **mystery shoppers**, spotters pose as anonymous customers but, during their unannounced visits, they observe workers carefully and later report to management any unusual or inappropriate behavior by bartenders or service staff.

- To control drink production, it is also important to designate drink portion size and the proper glassware to be used. This helps ensure that the portion size of the drink is appropriate and consistent with the guest's visual perception of a full glass. The ice to be used in drinks is also important for controlling drink production.

- Alcohol is a highly desirable product for many employees; therefore, its direct theft is always a possibility. This is especially true in a beverage service area that is secluded or in which bartenders have direct access to product inventory and ease of exit.

- Theft may also occur in the area of receptions and special events. Proper controls as well as strict rules limiting the access of employees to beer, wine, and liquor storage areas should help deter and detect theft of beverages.

- **Open bars (hosted bars)** are those in which no charge is made to guests for the individual drinks they consume but, when the bar is closed, one total amount is charged to the host or sponsor of the open bar.

- Bartenders who work open bars should be specially trained to spot signs of guest intoxication. As difficult as it may sometimes be, guests should be made aware that it is illegal, in all states, to serve an intoxicated guest. To do so puts the entire food and beverage operation at risk.

7. Optimizing Overall Cost of Sales Percentage

- While it is important to guard against inappropriate cost cutting, management can find itself in a position where food and beverage production costs must be reduced.

- The food cost percentage equation is deceptively easy to understand. In its simplest form, it can be represented as:

$$\frac{A}{B} = C$$

where

A = Cost of products sold
B = Sales
C = Cost percentage

- In general, the rules of algebra state the following about the $A/B = C$ formula:

  1. If A is unchanged and B increases, C decreases.
  2. If A is unchanged and B decreases, C increases.
  3. If A increases at the same proportional rate B increases, C remains unchanged.
  4. If A decreases while B is unchanged, C decreases.
  5. If A increases and B is unchanged, C increases.

- Put into foodservice management terms, these five algebraic statements can be translated, as follows:

  1. If costs can be kept constant but sales increase, the cost percentage goes down.
  2. If costs remain constant but sales decline, the cost percentage increases.
  3. If costs go up at the same rate sales go up, the cost of goods sold percentage will remain unchanged.
  4. If costs can be reduced while sales remain constant, the cost percentage goes down.
  5. If costs increase with no increase in sales, the cost percentage will go up.

- The six different basic approaches managers may consider when seeking to reduce their operations' overall product cost percentages are:
  1. Ensure that all products purchased are sold.
  2. Decrease portion size relative to price.
  3. Vary recipe composition.
  4. Alter product quality.
  5. Achieve a more favorable sales mix.
  6. Increase price relative to portion size.

- When managers find that an appropriate ingredient, rather than the highest-cost ingredient, provides good quality and good value to guests, product costs may be able to be reduced using product substitution. But recall that managers must be very careful in this area.

- Lower-quality products may cost an operator less, but customers may also perceive that menu items made from these lower-quality ingredients provide reduced levels of value to them and that reaction by guests must always be avoided.

- **Sales mix** is defined as the series of guest purchasing decisions that result in a specific food or beverage cost percentage. Sales mix affects overall product cost percentage anytime guests have a choice among several menu selections, each selection having its own unique product cost percentage.

- Managers can directly help to influence guest selection and sales mix by such techniques as strategic pricing, effective menu design, and creative marketing, but for a single operating day, it will always be the guests who will determine an operation's overall cost percentage. This is so because it is customers and their daily menu choices that determine an operations' sales mix.

- The use of effective marketing and promotion of good (lower product cost) items can help you influence sales mix in a favorable way, thus reducing your product cost percentage, and increasing your profitability, while allowing the portion size, recipe composition, and product quality of your menu items to remain constant.

8. Technology Tools

- In the past, restaurants were slow to install working computer terminals and other technological tools in kitchen areas where production staff could easily use them. Increasingly, however, these installations are being made. In a professional kitchen, cost control efforts are often shared between management and the production staff. Advanced technology programs available for kitchen production use include those that can help both you and your production staff members:

  1. Perform nutrition-related analysis of menu items including:
     - Recipe nutrient analysis
     - Diet analysis
     - FDA (Food and Drug Administration) food labels
     - Diabetic exchange
     - Weight management components
  2. Calculate total recipe costs and per portion costs.
  3. Compute product yield and product waste percentages.
  4. Compute actual versus ideal costs based on product issues.
  5. Estimate and compute daily food cost.

6. Maintain product usage records by:
    - Vendor
    - Product
    - Food category
    - Individual menu item
    - Ingredient
7. Compare portions served to portions produced to monitor over portioning and waste.
8. Report food and beverage product usage variances based on actual sales.
9. Suggest usage for carryover products.
10. Conduct "make versus buy" calculations on convenience items to optimize employee productivity and minimize costs.

Key Terms & Concepts Review
Match the key terms with their correct definitions.

1. Cost of sales   _____

   a. The portion cost of an item after cooking, trimming, portioning, or cleaning.

2. Food cost percentage   _____

   b. An individual employed by management for the purpose of inconspicuously observing bartenders and waitstaff in order to detect any fraudulent or policy-violating behavior.

3. Beginning inventory   _____

   c. Free or reduced-cost meals that are employee benefits and are labor-related, not food-related, costs.

4. Padding inventory   _____

   d. The sum of the beginning inventory and purchases. It represents the value of all food that was available for sale during the accounting period.

5. Purchases   _____

   e. The series of consumer-purchasing decisions that result in a specific food and beverage cost percentage.

6. Food available for sale   _____

   f. A bar in which no charge for an individual drink is made to the customer, thus establishing an all-you-can-drink environment.

7. Goods available for sale   _____

   g. Cost of goods sold figure that should be achievable given the product sales mix of a particular operation.

8. Ending inventory   _____

   h. A record of the ingredient costs required to produce an item sold by a foodservice operation.

9. Cost of food consumed   _____

   i. The combined value of the food and beverage costs used to produce a known quantity of revenue in a defined accounting period.

10. Employee meal cost _____	j.	The dollar value of all products on hand at the beginning of the accounting period. This amount is determined by completing a physical inventory.
11. Cost of food sold _____	k.	The sum value of the beginning inventory of food and all food purchases made by an operation during a defined accounting period.
12. Cost of beverage sold _____	l.	This term refers to the weight or count of a product as delivered to the foodservice operator.
13. Beverage cost percentage _____	m.	The portion of food sales that was spent on food expenses.
14. Standardized recipe cost sheet _____	n.	An individual employed by management to pose as an anonymous customer who, during an unannounced visit, observes an operation and reports the observations back to management.
15. As purchased (AP) _____	o.	The term used to describe the inappropriate activity of adding a value for nonexistent inventory items to the value of total inventory in an effort to understate actual costs.
16. Edible portion (EP) _____	p.	The dollar amount of all food actually sold, thrown away, wasted, or stolen, plus or minus transfers from other units, minus employee meals.
17. Yield test _____	q.	This formula is defined as one minus waste percentage and refers to the amount of product available for use by the operator after all preparation-related losses have been taken into account.
18. Butcher's yield test _____	r.	A calculation used to measure an operation's attainable product costs to its actual product cost.

19. Waste percentage	_____	s.	The actual dollar value of all food used by an operation in a specific time period.
20. Yield percentage	_____	t.	The ratio of an operation's beverage costs to its beverage sales.
21. Attainable product cost	_____	u.	The value of all beverage products sold, as well as the costs of all beverages given away, wasted, or stolen in a defined accounting period.
22. Operational efficiency ratio	_____	v.	A procedure designed to identify losses due to the trimming of inedible fat and bones in meat as well as losses due to the meat's cooking or slicing.
23. Head size	_____	w.	The dollar value of all products on hand at the end of the accounting period. This amount is determined by completing a physical inventory.
24. Hydrometer	_____	x.	An arrangement in which no charge is made to guests for the individual drinks they consume at an event but, when the bar is closed, one total amount is charged to the event's host or sponsor.
25. Spotter	_____	y.	This term refers to the weight or count of a product after it has been trimmed, cooked, and portioned.
26. Mystery shopper	_____	z.	An instrument used to measure the specific gravity of a liquid.
27. Open bar	_____	aa.	This formula is defined as product loss divided by AP weight and refers to product lost in the preparation process.
28. Hosted bar	_____	bb.	The amount of space on the top of a glass of beer that is made up of foam.

29. Sales mix _____

cc. A procedure used to determine actual EP ingredient costs. It is used to help establish actual costs on a product that will experience weight or volume loss in preparation.

30. Edible portion cost _____
    (EP cost)

dd. The sum cost of all food purchased during the accounting period. Determined by adding all properly tabulated invoices for the accounting period.

Discussion Questions

1. Explain the importance to managers of being able to calculate their cost of goods sold and their cost of goods sold percentages.

_____

_____

_____

_____

2. What is the primary difference between the two formulas managers use to calculate their cost of food sold and their cost of beverages sold?

_____

_____

_____

_____

3. List three questions that must be answered when determining actual and attainable product costs.

_____

_____

_____

_____

4. Identify the five types of product theft that managers must guard against when they operate a facility that serves alcoholic beverages.

_____

_____

_____

_____

5. List the six actions managers can take to reduce overall product cost percentage.

_____

_____

_____

_____

Quiz Yourself

Choose the letter of the best answer to the questions listed below.

1. When using the *USAR,* an operation's cost of sales is equal to its
   a. total controllable costs.
   b. food and beverage costs.
   c. food, beverage and labor costs.
   d. food, beverage, labor and occupancy costs.

2. In how many different ways would an operation's cost of sales typically be reported on the operation's P&L?
   a. 2
   b. 3
   c. 4
   d. 5

3. An operation's beginning inventory plus its purchases are equal to its
   a. total sales.
   b. ending inventory.
   c. cost of food consumed.
   d. goods available for sale.

4. What is the cost of food sold if an operation's Beginning Inventory equals $15,000, Ending Inventory equals $12,000, Purchases equal $11,500, and Employee Meals equal $1,500?
   a. $12,500
   b. $13,000
   c. $13,500
   d. $14,000

5. What is the formula that managers use to calculate a food cost percentage?
   a. Cost of food sold + Food sales = Food cost %
   b. Cost of food sold – Food sales = Food cost %
   c. Cost of food sold × Food sales = Food cost %
   d. Cost of food sold ÷ Food sales = Food cost %

6. How will an operation's costs be affected if its managers do not subtract employee meal costs from cost of food consumed when calculating their expenses?
   a. Cost of food and cost of labor would be overstated
   b. Cost of food and cost of labor would be understated
   c. Cost of food would be understated and cost of labor would be overstated
   d. Cost of food would be overstated and cost of labor would be understated

7. What was an operation's beverage cost % if its beverage sales were $37,500, Beginning Inventory was $14,500, Ending Inventory was $12,000, and Purchases were $5,000?
   a. 20.0%
   b. 22.5%
   c. 24.0%
   d. 26.5%

8. What were an operation's total beverage sales for an accounting period if its cost of beverages was $9,000 and its beverage cost percentage was 15 percent?
   a. $6,000
   b. $13,500
   c. $60,000
   d. $73,500

9. What was an operation's cost of beverages if beverage sales were $90,000 and beverage cost percentage was 20%?
   a. $1,980
   b. $4,500
   c. $19,800
   d. $45,000

10. What was an operation's beverage cost percentage if its beverage sales were $62,500, Beginning Inventory was $24,000, Ending Inventory was $22,000, and Purchases were $15,000?
    a. 19.1%
    b. 19.6%
    c. 20.1%
    d. 20.6%

11. The amount of an operation's beginning beverage inventory for an accounting period is exactly equal to the operation's
    a. cost of beverage sold for the current accounting period.
    b. ending beverage inventory for the previous accounting period.
    c. beginning beverage inventory for the previous accounting period.
    d. cost of beverage sold minus employee meals for the current accounting period.

12. Properly accounting for a product transfer from the bar to the kitchen will increase an operation's bar cost percentage and reduce its food cost percentage.
    a. True
    b. False

13. What will be the effect on product costs if a manager neglects to make a $300 transfer from the bar to the kitchen for alcohol used in the preparation of a red wine reduction sauce served over steaks?
    a. Beverage costs will be over stated and food costs will be under stated.
    b. Beverage costs will be under stated and food costs will be under stated.
    c. Beverage costs will be over stated and food costs will be over stated.
    d. Beverage costs will be under stated and food costs will be over stated.

14. An operation had beverage sales of $8,000 and food sales of $30,000. The operation's beverage cost before transfers was 20% and its food cost was 30%. A transfer of $400 was made from food cost to beverage cost. What was the operation's beverage cost percentage after this transfer was made?
    a. 20%
    b. 25%
    c. 30%
    d. 35%

15. Last month, a manager's submarine sandwich shop had meat cost of $11,525, produce cost of $1,875, bread costs of $2,100 and all other food-related costs of $4,500. What was the bread cost proportion of this manager's total product cost?
    a. 6.5%
    b. 8.5%
    c. 10.5%
    d. 12.5%

16. What assumption must managers make if they are to consider a six-column today/to-date food cost estimate to be accurate?
    a. Purchases are greater than ending inventory.
    b. Purchases and beginning inventory are equal.
    c. Beginning inventory is greater than ending inventory.
    d. Beginning inventory and ending inventory are equal.

17. How many pints are contained in one quart?
    a. 2
    b. 4
    c. 6
    d. 8

18. Which is the formula used to calculate a product's waste percentage?
    a. Product loss × AP weight
    b. Product loss × EP weight
    c. Product loss ÷ AP weight
    d. Product loss ÷ EP weight

19. A manager purchases an ingredient that has a known yield of 63 percent. The manager's recipe requires 5 pounds EP of this ingredient. Rounded to the nearest pound, what is the AP required amount of the ingredient the manager must buy to produce the recipe?
    a. 6 pounds
    b. 8 pounds
    c. 12 pounds
    d. 14 pounds

20. A manager purchases whole ducks for $2.28 a pound. After cleaning and trimming, the waste percentage for the ducks is 24 percent. What is the EP cost per pound for duck?
    a. $2.50
    b. $3.00
    c. $9.00
    d. $9.50

21. A facility's operational efficiency ratio is equal to its
    a. Actual product cost ÷ Attainable product cost.
    b. Actual product cost × Attainable product cost.
    c. Cost as per standardized recipes ÷ Attainable product cost.
    d. Cost as per standardized recipes × Attainable product cost.

22. A manager incurred actual product costs of $69,600 but had previously calculated her attainable product cost to be $58,000. What was the manager's actual cost % variance?
    a. 18%
    b. 20%
    c. 22%
    d. 24%

23. The purpose of a professional spotter in a food and beverage operation is to
    a. improve guest service levels.
    b. detect errors in beverage deliveries.
    c. detect inappropriate employee behavior.
    d. improve the results of butcher yield tests.

24. In the A/B = C formula for product cost, if A is unchanged, and B increases, C decreases.
    a. True
    b. False

25. In the A/B = C formula for product cost, if A increases and B is unchanged, C decreases.
    a. True
    b. False

26. If costs remain constant and sales decline, an operation's cost percentage will also decline.
    a. True
    b. False

27. If costs can be reduced while sales remain constant, an operation's cost percentage will also be reduced.
    a. True
    b. False

28. On any given day, the individuals most responsible for determining an operation's sales mix are its guests.
    a. True
    b. False

Chapter Answers to Key Terms & Concepts Review, Discussion Questions, and Quiz Yourself

Key Terms & Concepts Review

1. i	6. k	11. p	16. y	21. g	26. n
2. m	7. d	12. u	17. cc	22. r	27. f
3. j	8. w	13. t	18. v	23. bb	28. x
4. o	9. s	14. h	19. aa	24. z	29. e
5. dd	10. c	15. l	20. q	25. b	30. a

Discussion Questions

1. Explain the importance to managers of being able to calculate their cost of goods sold and their cost of goods sold percentages.

   - An operation's food and beverage costs are generally reported in two ways; (1) as a total dollar amount and (2) as a percentage of the operation's total sales. In nearly all foodservice operations, a manager's ability to control cost of sales will be used as a primary measure of that manager's competence and his or her abilities.
   - When managers can accurately calculate their cost of goods sold and their cost of goods sold percentages, they are in a good position to predict their operation's future performance in these areas.
   - When managers can predict (and budget for) their future costs, they can then compare their actual costs with their cost projections. When significant differences exist between forecasted performance and actual performance, managers can take the steps necessary to address those differences and to correct them.

2. What is the primary difference between the two formulas managers use to calculate their cost of food sold and their cost of beverages sold?

   - When calculating their cost of food sold, managers make a transfer "out" of cost of food consumed, and "into" labor costs, to account for the expense of employee meals.
   - When managers calculate their cost of beverages sold, they do not make a similar transfer because in nearly all operations the consumption of alcohol by employees while at work is prohibited.

3. List three questions that must be answered when determining actual and attainable product costs.

- What are our actual product costs?
- What should our product costs be?
- How close are we to this attainable goal?

4. Identify the five types of product theft that managers must guard against when they operate a facility that serves alcoholic beverages.

- Order filled but not rung up
- Overpouring or underpouring
- Dilution of product (watering down the drinks)
- Improper product substitution
- Direct theft

5. List the six actions managers can take to reduce overall product cost percentage.

- Ensure that all product purchased are sold.
- Decrease portion size relative to price.
- Vary recipe composition.
- Adjust product quality.
- Achieve a more favorable sales mix.
- Increase price relative to portion size.

Quiz Yourself

1. b.	8. c.	15. c.	22. b.
2. a.	9. c.	16. d.	23. c.
3. d.	10. a.	17. a.	24. a.
4. b.	11. b.	18. c.	25. b.
5. d.	12. b.	19. b.	26. b.
6. d.	13. a.	20. b.	27. a.
7. a.	14. b.	21. a.	28. a.

Chapter 6

Managing Food and Beverage Pricing

Learning Outcomes

At the conclusion of this chapter, you will be able to:

- Choose the best menu format for a specific foodservice operation.

    Menus are one of the best ways for managers to communicate directly with their customers. In the foodservice industry the term "menu" means both the items available for sale to guests and the way those items are communicated to guests.

    Managers preparing their operations' menus can choose from several different menu formats, each of which may be appropriate for a specific business and its customers. As a result, it is important that a manager knows how to choose the proper menu format for the facility he or she is in charge of operating. When managers make the proper menu format selection, their customers' satisfaction is enhanced and their operations' financial performance can be optimized.

- Identify the variables to be considered when establishing menu prices.

    Most managers recognize that there is a direct relationship between the cost of preparing a menu item and that menu item's selling price. It is always true that portion cost and portion size are significant factors that influence the price of a menu item. There are, however, a significant number of additional factors that can directly influence an operation's menu prices.

    Some of these additional factors can be controlled by managers but some cannot. Because that is true, it is important that managers know about each of these factors and how they can affect the prices that managers can charge to their customers.

- Assign menu prices to menu items based on the items' cost, popularity, and profitability.

    One of the most critical skills that must be mastered by foodservice managers is that of knowing how to calculate appropriate prices for the products they sell. Even for those managers in facilities such as hospitals and university housing units that may not assign prices to individual menu items, understanding how overall selling prices based on item cost, popularity, and profitability directly affect customers and the financial performance foodservice operations is essential.

Study Notes

1. Menu Formats

- Menus are one of the most effective ways managers can use to communicate with their guests. The menu also provides an excellent opportunity to build impulse sales or to communicate special sales and services the facility has to offer.

- Menus in foodservice establishments generally fall into one of three major categories: standard, daily, and cycle.

- Menu **tip-ons**, which are smaller menu segments clipped on to more permanent menus, can prove very effective in influencing impulse buying.

- The **standard menu** is printed, displayed, recited by service staff, or otherwise communicated to the guest. The standard menu is fixed day after day, simplifies the ordering process; guests tend to have a good number of choices, and guest preference data (percent of guests selecting each item available for sale) can be easily obtained.

- But, standard menus often do not utilize carryovers effectively, cannot be used to respond quickly to market price changes of offered items, and do not allow easy seasonal adjustments of menu items.

- The **daily menu** changes every day. Management can respond quickly to changes in ingredient or item prices, and can use carryovers.

- But, daily menu planning is more difficult; as is collecting customer data regarding buying behavior is more complex.

- A **cycle menu** is a menu in effect for a specific time period. The length of the cycle refers to the length of time the menu is in effect. Typically, cycle menus are repeated regularly; often on a weekly or monthly basis. Production personnel can be trained to produce a wider variety of foods with a cycle menu than with a standard menu.

- With cycle menus, purchasing is simplified, proper inventory levels are easy to maintain and carryovers are easily utilized.

2. Menu Specials

- Regardless of the menu type used, you can generally incorporate minor menu changes on a regular basis.

- Minor menu changes can be accomplished through the offering of daily or weekly **menu specials**—that is, menu items that will appear on the menu as you desire and then removed when they are either consumed or discontinued.

- Daily or weekly menu specials provide variety, low-cost raw ingredients, carryover utilization, or test-market potential for new menu items.

- The menu special is a powerful cost control tool.

3. Factors Affecting Menu Pricing

- It is important to remember that revenue and price are not synonymous terms.

- **Revenue** means the amount spent by *all guests* while **Price** refers to the amount charged to *one guest*. Total revenue is generated by the following formula:

$$\text{Price} \times \text{Number sold} = \text{Total revenue}$$

- As price increases, the number of items sold by a business will generally decrease.

- Guests demand a good **price/value relationship** when making their purchases.

- The price/value relationship reflects guests' view of how much value they are receiving for the prices they are paying.

- Price can be significantly affected by all of the following factors:

Factors Influencing Menu Price
1. Economic conditions
2. Local competition
3. Service levels
4. Guest type
5. Product quality
6. Portion size
7. Ambience
8. Meal period
9. Location
10. Sales mix

- The economic conditions that exist in a local area or even in an entire country can have a significant impact on the prices restaurant managers can charge for their menu items. When an economy is robust and growing, managers generally have a greater ability to charge higher prices for the items they sell.

- While it is important to understand what competitors charge for their items, successful foodservice operators spend their time focusing on building guest value in their *own* operations, and not in attempting to mimic the efforts of the competition.

- Guests expect to pay more for the same product when service levels are higher. Because service levels impact pricing directly, as the personal level of service increases in an operation, selling prices may also be increased.

- Some guests are simply less price sensitive than others. All guests, however, want value for their money.

- Foodservice operators should select the quality level that best represents their guests' anticipated desire as well as their goals, and then price the products accordingly. Visual product quality and grade of ingredients, as well as portion size and service level, are factors that impact a guest's view of overall product quality.

- Portion size plays a large role in determining menu pricing. It is a function of both product quantity and presentation. The proper dish size is just as critical as the proper size of scoop or ladle when serving the food.

- For the foodservice operator who provides an attractive ambience, menu prices can be increased. However, excellent product quality with outstanding service goes much further over the long run than do clever restaurant designs.

- In some cases, diners expect to pay more for an item served in the evening than for that same item served at a lunch period. You must exercise caution in this area. Guests should clearly understand *why* a menu item's price changes with the time of day.

- An operation's location can be a major factor in determining its prices.

- There is no discounting the value of a prime restaurant location. Even the best location, however, does not guarantee success.

- In fact, location can be an asset or a liability. If it is an asset, menu prices may reflect that fact. If location is indeed a liability, menu prices may actually need to be lower to attract a sufficient clientele to ensure the operation achieves its total revenue and profit goals.

- Sales mix (see Chapter 5) refers to the specific menu items selected by guests when they visit an operation.

- Sales mix will heavily influence the menu pricing decision, just as guest purchase decisions will influence total product costs.

- **Price blending** refers to the process of pricing products, with very different individual cost percentages, in groups with the intent of achieving a favorable overall cost situation.

- Recall from Chapter 5 that the formula for computing food cost percentage is:

$$\frac{\text{Cost of food sold}}{\text{Food sales}} = \text{Food cost \%}$$

- This formula can be worded somewhat differently for a single menu item without changing its accuracy:

$$\frac{\text{Cost of a specific food item sold}}{\text{Food sales of that item}} = \text{Food cost \% of that item}$$

- It is important to understand that the "food sales of that item" in the above formula is synonymous with the selling price when evaluating the menu price of a single menu item. The principles of algebra allow you to rearrange the formula as follows:

$$\frac{\text{Cost of a specific food item sold}}{\text{Food cost \% of that item}} = \text{Food sales (selling price) of that item}$$

4. Assigning Menu Prices

- In general, menu prices are most often assigned on the basis of one of the following two concepts: product cost percentage or contribution margin.

- The **product cost percentage** approach to menu item pricing is based on the idea that the product cost (portion cost) of a menu item should be a predetermined percentage of the item's selling price.

- When management uses a predetermined food cost percentage to price menu items, it is stating its belief that product cost in relationship to selling price is of great importance.

- To aid in pricing items, a cost factor or multiplier can be assigned to each desired food cost percentage as follows:

$$\frac{1.00}{\text{Desired product cost \%}} = \text{Pricing factor}$$

- The pricing factor, when multiplied by any product cost, will result in a selling price that yields the appropriate menu price. The formula is as follows:

$$\text{Pricing factor} \times \text{Product cost} = \text{Menu price}$$

- A **plate cost** is simply the sum of all product costs included in a single meal (or "plate") as served to a guest. The proper calculation of a plate cost is important when more than one menu item is included for one price. A simple example is that of a steak sold with a baked potato accompaniment for single price.

- Some managers prefer to use a desired contribution margin when establishing their prices rather than a targeted food cost percentage.

- **Contribution margin** is defined as the amount that remains after the product cost of a menu item is subtracted from the menu item's selling price.

- Contribution margin is computed as follows:

> Selling price – Product cost = Contribution margin

- When this approach is used, the formula for determining selling price is:

> Product cost + Contribution margin desired = Selling price

- The effective manager will view pricing as an important process with an end goal of setting a good price/value relationship in the mind of the guest.

- Regardless of whether the pricing method used is based on achieving a desired food cost percentage or achieving a targeted contribution margin, the selling price selected must provide for a predetermined operational profit.

5. Special Pricing Situations

- Some pricing decisions faced by foodservice managers call for a unique approach. In many cases, pricing is used as a way to influence guests' purchasing decisions or to respond to particularly complex situations. The following are examples of special pricing situations and issues:

  - Coupons
  - Value pricing
  - Bundling
  - Salad bars and buffets
  - Bottled wine
  - Beverages at receptions and parties.

- Coupons are a popular way to vary menu price. There are basically two types of coupons in use in the hospitality industry. The first type allows guests to get a free item when they buy another item. This is known as the "buy one get one" or **BOGO** approach to couponing.

112

- With the second type of coupon, some form of restriction is placed on the coupon's use. For example, the coupon may only be accepted at a certain time of day, or a reduction in price granted by the coupon's use may be available only if the guest purchases a specific designated menu item.

- Coupons have the effect of reducing sales revenue from each guest in the hope that the total number of guests will increase to the point that total sales revenue increases.

- **Value pricing** refers to the practice of reducing prices on selected menu items in the belief that, as in couponing, total guest counts will increase to the point that total sales revenue also increases.

- **Bundling** refers to the practice of selecting specific menu items and pricing them as a group in such a manner that the single menu price of the group is lower than if the items in the group were purchased individually.

- With bundling, as with couponing or value pricing, lower menu prices are accepted by management in the belief that this pricing strategy will increase total sales revenue and thus profit, by increasing the number of guests served.

- The difficulty in establishing a set price for either a salad bar or buffet is that total portion cost can vary greatly from one guest to the next.

- Total food costs on a buffet line or salad bar are a function of two things:
  - How much is eaten
  - What is eaten

- One secret to keeping the selling price low in a salad bar or buffet is to apply the ABC inventory approach (see Chapter 4). That is, A items should comprise no more than 20 percent of the total product available; B items, no more than 30 percent; and C items, 50 percent.

- Managers use the following formula to determine buffet product cost per guest:

$$\frac{\text{Total buffet product cost}}{\text{Guests served}} = \text{Buffet product cost per guest}$$

- Few areas of menu pricing create more controversy than that of pricing wines by the bottle. The reason for this may be the incredible variance in cost among different **vintages** or years of production, as well as the quality of alternative wine offerings.

- Many beverage managers prefer to focus on contribution margin when selling bottled wines rather than product cost percentage.

- How you decide to price the bottled wine offerings on your menu will affect your guests' perception of the price/value relationship offered by your operation.

- **Price spread** is defined as the range (spread) between the lowest and highest priced menu item.

- Pricing beverages for open-bar events can be difficult, since each consumer group (each group of guests attending a function) can be expected to behave somewhat differently when attending an open bar or hosted bar function.

- When charging on a per person, per-hour basis you must have a good idea of how much the average attendee will consume during the length of the party or reception so that an appropriate price can be established.

- Maintaining records of beverage consumption during past events and calculations of average consumption patterns for each guest type group helps managers establish appropriate prices for beverages served during receptions.

5. Technology Tools

- In this chapter, you will have learned about the menu formats you will most often encounter as a hospitality manager, as well as the factors affecting menu prices and the procedures used to assign individual menu item prices based on cost and historical sales data.

- The mathematical computations required to evaluate the effectiveness of individual menu items and to establish their prices can be complex, but there are a wide range of software products available that can help you to:

  1. Develop menus and cost recipes.
  2. Design and print menu "specials" for meal periods or happy hours.
  3. Compute and analyze menu item and overall food cost percentage.
  4. Compute and analyze menu item and overall contribution margin.
  5. Price banquet menus and bars based on known product costs.
  6. Evaluate the profitability of individual menu items.

7. Estimate future item demand based on past purchase patterns.
8. Assign individual menu item prices based on management-supplied parameters.

- Menu analysis and pricing software is often packaged as part of a larger software program. It is an area that will continue to see rapid development in the future as software makers seek additional ways to improve their products.

Key Terms & Concepts Review
Match the key terms with their correct definitions.

1. Tip-on _____

    a. A menu that is in effect for a predetermined length of time, such as 7 days or 14 days.

2. Standard menu _____

    b. The practice of reducing all or most prices on the menu in the belief that total guest counts will increase to the point that total sales revenue also increases.

3. Daily menu _____

    c. Menu items that will appear on the menu and be removed when they are either consumed or discontinued. These daily or weekly specials are an effort to provide variety, take advantage of low-cost raw ingredients, utilize carryover products, or test market potential of new menu items.

4. À la carte (menu) _____

    d. The guests' view of how much value they are receiving for the price they are paying.

5. Prix fixe (menu) _____

    e. The feeling or overall mood created in an operation by its decor, staff uniforms, music and other factors that directly affect its atmosphere.

6. Cycle menu _____

    f. The sum cost of all product costs included in a single meal (or "plate") served to a guest for one fixed price.

7. CEO (chief executive officer) _____

    g. A menu format in which guests select individual menu items and each menu item is priced separately.

8. Menu specials _____

    h. The difference in price on a menu between the lowest and highest priced item of a similar nature.

9. Selling price   _____

     i. The process of assigning prices based on product groups for the purpose of achieving predetermined cost objectives.

10. Price/value relationship   _____

     j. A small menu segment clipped to a larger and more permanent list of menu items.

11. Ambience   _____

     k. The practice of selecting specific menu items and pricing them as a group; in such a manner that the single menu price of the group is lower than if the items comprising the group were purchased individually.

12. Price blending   _____

     l. The specific year(s) of production for a wine.

13. Plate cost   _____

     m. A menu that changes every day.

14. Contribution margin   _____

     n. A menu format in which guests select a preset group of menu items and then pay one set (fixed) price for all of the menu items included in the grouping.

15. Buy one, get one (BOGO)   _____

     o. The total amount paid by guests for the purchase of a singly priced item.

16. Value pricing   _____

     p. The profit or margin that remains after product cost is subtracted from an item's selling price.

17. Bundling   _____

     q. A printed and otherwise fixed menu that stays the same day after day.

18. Vintage   _____

     r. The highest-ranking leader/manager in an organization.

19. Price spread   _____

     s. A marketing technique in which buyers who purchase a single item receive a second and identical item for no additional charge.

Discussion Questions

1. Identify and explain the three major menu formats used by managers.

   _____

   _____

   _____

   _____

2. List the nine factors that can influence menu price.

   _____

   _____

   _____

   _____

3. Explain why some managers employ the strategies of price "blending" and of product "bundling."

   _____

   _____

   _____

   _____

4. List and explain the two basic methods that managers use when assigning menu prices.

   _____

   _____

   _____

   _____

5. Identify and explain four of the six special pricing situations managers may encounter.

   _____

   _____

   _____

   _____

Quiz Yourself

Choose the letter of the best answer to the questions listed below.

1. Which menu format would be best used by the manager of a facility where guests will eat each of their daily meals, seven days every week, and for a period of one year, in that manager's facility?
   a. cycle
   b. daily
   c. standard
   d. prix fixe

2. The most important characteristic of a menu tip-on is its ability to
   a. reduce menu prices.
   b. reduce service times.
   c. create customer impulse buys.
   d. create a lesser need for physical menus.

3. Which menu format can best take advantage of seasonal items available only for short periods of time?
   a. cycle
   b. daily
   c. standard
   d. prix fixe

4. It is most difficult to obtain meaningful customer preference data from which menu format?
   a. cycle
   b. daily
   c. standard
   d. prix fixe

5. Which menu format is most popular in commercial restaurants?
   a. cycle
   b. daily
   c. standard
   d. prix fixe

6. Which menu format is most popular in noncommercial and institutional foodservice settings?
   a. cycle
   b. daily
   c. standard
   d. prix fixe

7. With which menu type do customers pay one price for a complete meal?
   a. cycle
   b. daily
   c. standard
   d. prix fixe

8. Menu specials can be effective regardless of the type of menu format utilized in a foodservice operation.
   a. True
   b. False

9. Once added, menu specials should not be removed from the menu.
   a. True
   b. False

10. Menu specials can be useful in utilizing low-cost or seasonal raw ingredients.
    a. True
    b. False

11. Menu specials are a poor tool for testing the popularity of new menu items.
    a. True
    b. False

12. Menu specials are powerful cost control tools.
    a. True
    b. False

13. A manager prices a menu item at $10.99. The manager sells 510 servings of that item in a week. What was the manager's total revenue for the item in that week?
    a. $5,404.90
    b. $5,504.90
    c. $5,604.90
    d. $5,704.90

14. In the hospitality industry, it is most often true that as price
    a. decreases, the number of items sold decreases.
    b. increases, the number of items sold decreases.
    c. decreases, the number of items sold remains unchanged.
    d. increases, the number of items sold remains unchanged.

15. The portion cost for an item sold by a manager is $4.38. The manager sells the menu item for $10.95. What is this item's food cost percentage?
    a. 25%
    b. 30%
    c. 35%
    d. 40%

16. The portion cost for an item sold by a manager is $4.28. The manager wants to sell the item to achieve a 25 percent food cost. What should be this menu item's selling price?
    a. $14.12
    b. $15.12
    c. $16.12
    d. $17.12

17. The process of pricing products with varying cost percentages in a group to achieve a favorable overall cost percentage is known as
    a. value pricing.
    b. price blending.
    c. prix fixe pricing.
    d. competitive pricing.

18. What is the pricing factor a manager should use if she wants to price a menu item to yield a 25 percent food cost?
    a. 3.0
    b. 3.5
    c. 4.0
    d. 4.5

19. The sum total of costs included in a single meal served to a guest is referred to as a
    a. plate cost.
    b. fixed cost.
    c. portion cost.
    d. contribution margin.

20. A manager wants a contribution margin of $4.50 for each entrée he sells. The manager's standardized recipe for his lasagna entrée yields 40 servings and cost $200.00 to make. What should be the manager's selling price for lasagna?
    a. $9.00
    b. $9.50
    c. $10.00
    d. $10.50

21. When calculated using a simple formula, contribution margin is equal to
    a. Selling price – Product cost.
    b. Product cost + Selling price.
    c. Pricing factor ÷ Product cost.
    d. Selling price × Pricing factor.

22. For managers using the contribution margin approach to pricing, selling price is equal to
    a. Pricing factor – Product cost.
    b. Desired contribution margin ÷ Product cost.
    c. Product cost × Contribution margin desired.
    d. Product cost + Contribution margin desired.

23. A manager's standardized recipe cost $89.60 to make. The recipe yields 40 servings. The manager sells the item made by the recipe for $9.95. What is this item's per portion contribution margin?
    a. $7.51
    b. $7.71
    c. $7.91
    d. $8.11

24. Which strategy refers to reducing selling price significantly on selected menu items for the purpose of increasing total revenue in an operation?
    a. Bundling
    b. Value pricing
    c. Factor pricing
    d. Contribution margin pricing

25. What pricing strategy is a manager using if she chooses to charge one price for a hamburger, French fry and soft drink combination, and the single price charged for this group of items is lower than the combined prices of each individual item if sold separately?
    a. Bundling
    b. Value pricing
    c. Factor pricing
    d. Contribution margin pricing

26. Managers can control buffet and salad bar costs when they recognize that these costs are affected by how much is eaten by guests and by
    a. who eats it.
    b. what is eaten.
    c. when it is eaten.
    d. the time it takes to eat it.

27. At the beginning of a buffet meal, a manager placed $2,400 worth of food on the buffet line. During the meal, another $1,800 of food was added to the line. At the end of the meal, the value of the remaining food was $500. What was the total product cost of the manager's buffet during this meal period?
   e. $3,200
   f. $3,700
   g. $4,200
   h. $4,700

28. A manager placed $840 worth of food on a salad bar at the beginning of service. During service, the manager added another $275 worth of food. At the end of service, the value of the remaining food on the salad bar was $115. On this day, 400 guests purchased the salad bar. What was the manager's per guest cost for the salad bar?
   i. $2.00
   j. $2.50
   k. $2.75
   l. $3.00

29. The difference between a menu's highest and lowest priced items is referred to as the menu's
   a. factor.
   b. portion cost.
   c. price spread.
   d. contribution margin.

30. A manager pays $7.00 per bottle for a particular type of wine. What would be the manager's product cost percentage if he sells that wine at a price that achieves his $21.00 per bottle contribution margin target?
   a. 25%
   b. 30%
   c. 35%
   d. 40%

31. At the beginning of a wedding reception, a manager stocks a hosted bar with $1,100 worth of beverages. During the reception, the manager added another $500 worth of beverages to the bar. At the end of the event, $400 worth of beverages remained unconsumed. 125 guests attended the reception. What was the manager's per guest cost for beverages during this reception?
   a. $5.60
   b. $7.60
   c. $9.60
   d. $11.60

Chapter Answers to Key Terms & Concepts Review, Discussion Questions, and Quiz Yourself

Key Terms & Concepts Review

1. j	6. a	11. e	16. b
2. q	7. r	12. i	17. k
3. m	8. c	13. f	18. l
4. g	9. o	14. p	19. h
5. n	10. d	15. s	

Discussion Questions

1. Identify and explain the three major menu formats used by managers.

   - Standard menu: This menu is printed, displayed, recited by service staff, or otherwise communicated to the guest. The menu is fixed day after day with the possibility of seasonal revisions.
   - Daily menu: This menu changes every day. This concept is popular in upscale restaurants. This menu allows the chef or manager maximum production flexibility.
   - Cycle menu: This menu is in effect for a specific time period. The length of the cycle refers to the length of time the menu is in effect. Typically, cycle menus are repeated on a regular basis. They are used most often in institutional settings such as universities, retirement centers, schools, correctional facilities, and hospitals.

2. List the nine factors that can influence menu price.

   - Local competition
   - Service levels
   - Guest type
   - Product quality
   - Portion size
   - Ambiance
   - Meal period
   - Location
   - Sales mix

3. Explain why some managers employ the strategies of price "blending" and of product "bundling."

- Managers employee price "blending" in an effort to ensure targeted food cost percentages for contribution margins are achieve a selling menu items of varying product costs. When utilizing blending, managers sell some high-cost items for lower prices and some low-cost items for higher prices.
- "Bundling" is a pricing strategy used by managers when they combine two or more menu items into a package, with the intent of encouraging customers to buy the package rather than just some of the items.

4. List and explain the two basic methods that managers use when assigning menu prices.

- The product cost percentage method of pricing is used when managers feel product cost should be a predetermined percentage of a selling price. When management uses a predetermined food cost percentage to price menu items, it is stating its belief that product cost in relationship to selling price is of vital importance.

- The product contribution margin method of pricing is used when managers feel the amount that remains after the product cost of the menu item is subtracted from the item's selling price is of most importance. When using this approach, the contribution margin is the amount remaining after paying for the product cost and that "contributes" to paying for labor and other expenses as well as for providing a profit.

5. Identify and explain four of the six special pricing situations managers may encounter.

- Coupons: Coupons are a popular way to vary menu price. There are two types of coupons in use in the hospitality industry. The first type generally allows the guest to get a free item when he or she buys another item. With the second type, some form of restriction is placed on the coupon's use.
- Value Pricing: Refers to the practice of reducing all or most prices on the menu in the belief that total guest counts will increase to the point that total sales revenue also increases.
- Bundling: Refers to the practice of selecting specific menu items and pricing them as a group, in such a manner that the single menu price of the group is lower than if the items comprising the group were purchased individually.
- Salad bars and buffets: The difficulty in establishing a set price for either a salad bar or a buffet is that total portion cost can vary

greatly from one guest to the next. A person weighing 100 pounds will eat a lot less than a person weighing 300 pounds. The secret to keeping the selling price low in a salad bar or buffet is to apply the ABC inventory approach. That is, *A* items should comprise no more than 20% of the total product available; *B* items, no more than 30%; and *C* items, 50%.

- Bottled wine: Few areas of menu pricing create more controversy than that of pricing wines by the bottle. The reason may be the incredible variance in cost among different vintages, or years of production. How you decide to price the bottled wine offerings on your menu will definitely affect your guest's perception of the price/value relationship offered by your operation.

- Beverages at receptions and parties: Pricing beverages for open-bar receptions and special events can be very difficult. One way to take care of this problem is to charge the guest for all the drinks he or she actually consumed. Also, maintaining past events and records of what the average consumption for each group of guests has been can help you establish an appropriate price.

Quiz Yourself

1. a.	9. b.	17. b.	25. a.
2. c.	10. a.	18. c.	26. b.
3. b.	11. b.	19. a.	27. a.
4. b.	12. a.	20. b.	28. b.
5. c.	13. c.	21. a.	29. c.
6. a.	14. b.	22. d.	30. a.
7. d.	15. c.	23. b.	31. c.
8. a.	16. d.	24. b.	

Chapter 7

Managing the Cost of Labor

Learning Outcomes

At the conclusion of this chapter, you will be able to:

- Identify the factors that affect employee productivity.

   High levels of worker productivity are important to the profitable operation of any foodservice facility. When workers are highly productive more work can be done in less time and for less money. There are a variety of factors that affect the productivity level of workers and work teams. Many of these factors are directly under the control of management.

   Good managers know and understand the factors that affect the productivity of their workforces, and how their own actions can make a positive contribution to enhancing the productivity of each of their workers. When they understand these factors and act on that knowledge, workforce productivity improves, labor costs decline, and profits will increase.

- Develop labor standards and employee schedules used in a foodservice operation.

   A labor standard is a management-established level of performance expected of employees. When a labor standard is used to develop employee schedules in an operation, that operation's labor budget can be maintained, guest service levels can be enhanced, and managers can assess the overall quality of their workforce's efforts.

   Managers established labor standards so they can compare the actual labor costs and productivity levels achieved within their operations with those costs and productivity levels they had planned to achieve.

- Analyze and evaluate actual labor utilization.

   Just as foodservice managers carefully analyze and evaluate their actual product usage, the best managers carefully analyze and evaluate their actual labor usage. When too much labor is used in an operation labor costs may be excessive. If too little labor is used, however, guest service levels may decline and operational quality may be reduced. To ensure an operation utilizes its labor in the most effective way managers carefully analyze and evaluate labor utilization. Learning to do this well is a skill that should be acquired by all effective managers.

127

Study Notes

1. Labor Expense in the Hospitality Industry

- In today's economy labor costs are constantly increasing, thus managers cannot simply overstaff in an effort to meet anticipated demand. Other methods must be used to accomplish all necessary tasks and stay within the allotted labor budget.

- In some foodservice establishments, the cost of labor actually exceeds the cost of food and beverage products.

- Today's shrinking workforce indicates that many managers will find it increasingly more difficult to recruit, train, and retain an effective and productive group of qualified employees.

- **Payroll** is the term used to refer to the salaries and wages paid to employees.

- **Labor expense** includes salaries and wages, but it consists of other labor-related costs as well.

- Items identified as a labor expense can vary somewhat from operation to operation, but will normally include such items as:

  - FICA taxes
  - FUTA (federal unemployment taxes)
  - State unemployment taxes
  - Worker's compensation
  - Group life insurance
  - Health insurance:
    - Medical
    - Dental
    - Vision
    - Disability
  - Pension/ retirement plan payments
  - Employee meals (see Chapter 5)
  - Employee training expense
  - Employee transportation costs
  - Employee uniforms, housing, and other benefits
  - Vacation/sick leave expenses
  - Tuition reimbursement programs
  - Employee incentives and bonuses

- Not every operation will incur all of the costs listed, but some operations will have all of these and more.

- Payroll actually refers to the *gross* pay received by an employee in exchange for his or her work. That is, if an employee earns $15.00 per hour and works 40 hours for his or her employer, the gross paycheck (the employee's paycheck before any mandatory or voluntary deductions) would be $600 ($15.00 per hour × 40 hours = $600). This gross amount is considered payroll expense.

- A **salaried employee** receives the same paid income per week or month, regardless of the number of hours he or she works.

- A salaried employee is actually more accurately described as an **exempt employee** because the employee's duties, responsibilities, and level of decisions make the person "exempt" from the overtime provisions of the federal government's Fair Labor Standards Act (FLSA).

- Some employees are needed simply to open the doors of an operation for the minimally anticipated business. **Minimum staff** is used to designate the least number of employees, or payroll dollars, needed to operate a facility or department within the facility.

- **Fixed payroll** refers to the amount an operation pays in salaries. It is most often the same from month to month.

- **Variable payroll** consists of those dollars paid to hourly employees.

- Variable payroll is added only when management feels it is necessary to provide extra employees in anticipation of an increase in the number of guests to be served.

- Management has little control over fixed labor expense, but nearly 100 percent control over variable labor expense.

- Unlike payroll expense, labor expense refers to the total of *all* costs associated with maintaining a foodservice workforce. As a result, total labor expense will always exceed that of payroll expense.

- Payroll is considered a *controllable* labor expense, unlike FICA taxes and insurance premiums. But, in reality, managers may even be able to influence some of their non-controllable labor expenses, such as providing a training program to reduce injuries and insurance premiums.

2. Evaluating Labor Productivity

- Productivity is the amount of work performed by an employee in a fixed period of time.

- There are many ways to assess labor productivity. In general, productivity is measured in terms of the **productivity ratio** as follows:

$$\frac{\text{Output}}{\text{Input}} = \text{Productivity ratio}$$

- There are several ways of defining foodservice output and input; thus, there are several types of productivity ratios.

- Productivity ratios can be helpful in determining the answer to a manager's key question, "How much should I spend on labor?"

- Foodservice operators must develop their own methods for managing payroll because every foodservice unit is different.

3. Maintaining a Productive Workforce

- The following are 10 key employee-related factors that affect employee productivity:

10 Key Factors Affecting Employee Productivity
1. Employee selection
2. Training
3. Supervision
4. Scheduling
5. Breaks
6. Morale
7. Menu
8. Convenience food use versus scratch preparation
9. Equipment/tools
10. Service level desired

- Choosing the right employee is vital in developing a highly productive workforce. The process begins with the development of the job description and job specification.

- A **job description** is a listing of the tasks that must be accomplished by the employee hired to fill a particular position.

- A **job specification** is a listing of the personal characteristics needed to perform the tasks contained in a particular job description.

- When actually beginning to select employees for vacancies, one or more of the following selection aids are normally used:

  - Applications
  - Interviews
  - Preemployment testing
  - Background/reference checks

- The **employment application** is a document completed by the candidate for employment.

- Job interviews, if improperly performed, can subject an employer to significant legal liability.

- The Equal Employment Opportunity Commission suggests that all employers consider the following three issues when deciding whether to include a particular question on an employment application or in a job interview:

  - Does this question tend to screen out minorities or females?
  - Is the answer needed to judge this individual's competence for performance of the job?
  - Are there alternative, nondiscriminatory ways to judge the person's qualifications?

- Preemployment testing is increasingly used as a tool for helping to choose better employees and thus improve employee productivity.

- **Skills tests** can include activities such as cooking tests, typing tests, and computer application tests.

- **Psychological testing** can include personality tests, tests designed to predict performance, or tests of mental ability.

- **Preemployment drug testing** is used to determine if an applicant uses illegal drugs.

- Increasingly, hospitality employers are also utilizing background checks prior to hiring employees in selected positions. Common verification points include the following:
  - Name
  - Social Security number
  - Address history
  - Dates of past employment and duties performed
  - Education/training
  - Criminal background
  - Credit history

- Failure to conduct background checks on some positions can subject the employer to potential litigation under the doctrine of **negligent hiring**, that is, a failure on the part of an employer to exercise reasonable care in the selection of employees.

- No area under management control holds greater promise for increased employee productivity than job improvement through training.

- Effective training will improve job satisfaction and instill in employees a sense of well-being and accomplishment. It will also reduce confusion, product waste, and loss of guests.

- Effective training begins with a good **orientation program**.

- Topics commonly addressed in an orientation program may include company policies and procedures related to:
  - Payday
  - Annual performance review
  - Probationary period
  - Dress code
  - Telephone call, cell phone use policy
  - Smoking policy
  - Uniform allowance
  - Disciplinary system
  - Educational assistance
  - Work schedule
  - Mandatory meetings
  - Tip policy
  - Transfers
  - Employee meal policy
  - Sexual harassment policy
  - Lockers/security
  - Jury duty
  - Leave of absence
  - Maternity leave

- Alcohol/drug policy
- Employee assistance programs
- Tardy policy
- Sick leave policy
- Vacation policy
- Holidays and holiday pay
- Overtime pay
- Insurance
- Retirement programs
- Safety/emergency procedures
- Grievance procedures

- **Task training** is the training undertaken to ensure an employee has the skills to meet established productivity goals.

- The first step in developing a training program is determining how the task is to be done. After a method for completing a task is developed, it should be strictly enforced unless a better way is later developed. Discipline should be administered positively.

- The second step in developing a training program is planning the training session. Taking time to plan the training sessions lets employees know that management is taking it seriously.

- The third step in developing a training program is presenting the training session. Present sessions with enthusiasm. Always make sure that training is presented not because employees "don't know" but rather because management wants them to "know more."

- The fourth step is evaluating the session's effectiveness. Evaluation can be as simple as observing employee behavior or as detailed as preparing written questions for answer by employees in the testing situation, but it must always be done to ensure the employees learned.

- The fifth and final step requires retraining at the proper intervals. Employees must be retrained and reminded of critical information on a regular basis if their productivity and skill levels are to remain high.

- All employees require proper supervision.

- Proper supervision means assisting employees in improving productivity.

- When supervision is geared toward helping, the guest benefits and, thus, the operation benefits. This is why it is so important for managers to be **on the floor**, in other words, in the dining area, during meal periods.

- When employees can please both the guests and the manager at the same time, productivity rises; if employees feel that they can only satisfy the guest *or* the operation, difficulties will arise.

- Even with highly productive employees, poor employee scheduling by management can result in low productivity ratios.

- Proper scheduling ensures that the correct number of employees is available to do the necessary amount of work.

- Scheduling efficiency can often be improved through the use of the **split-shift**, a technique used to match individual employee work shifts with peaks and valleys of customer demand.

- Employees have both a physical and a mental need for breaks from their work. Management should view breaks as a necessary part of maintaining a highly productive workforce, not as lost or wasted time.

- Employees need to know that management cares enough to establish a reasonable employee break schedule and that management will stick to it.

- Management must create a fun, motivating environment for employees to work in.

- Motivated groups usually work for a management team that has created a vision, communicated the vision to employees, and ensured that employees share the vision.

- Creating a vision is nothing more than finding a "purpose" for the workforce.

- A shared purpose between management and employees is important for the development and maintenance of high morale.

- Employee turnover *is* high in some sections of the hospitality industry. By some estimates, it exceeds 200 percent per year. You can measure your turnover by using the following formula:

$$\frac{\text{Number of employees separated}}{\text{Number of employees in workforce}} = \text{Employee turnover rate}$$

- **Separated** is the term used to describe employees who have either quit, been terminated, or in some other manner have "separated" themselves from the operation.

- Some foodservice operators prefer to distinguish between voluntary and involuntary separation.

- A **voluntary separation** is one in which the employee made the decision to leave the organization.

- An **involuntary separation** is one in which management has caused the employee to separate from the organization.

- The basic turnover formula can be modified to create these two ratios:

$$\frac{\text{Number of employees involuntarily separated}}{\text{Number of employees in workforce}} = \text{Involuntary employee turnover rate}$$

$$\frac{\text{Number of employees voluntarily separated}}{\text{Number of employees in workforce}} = \text{Voluntary employee turnover rate}$$

- Turnover is expensive. This expense is comprised of actual and hidden costs. Actual costs include interviewing and training time, while hidden costs refer to the number of dishes broken by a new dishwasher, food wasted by new cooks, or even poor service levels that result in reduced sales levels.

- A major factor in employee productivity is the foodservice operation's actual menu.

- In general, the more variety of items a kitchen is asked to produce, the less efficient that kitchen will be.

- Menu items must also be selected to complement the skill level of the employees and the equipment available to produce the menu item.

- Since most foodservice operations change their menus infrequently, it is critical that the menu items selected can be prepared efficiently and well.

- The decision of whether to "make" or "buy" a convenience food item involves two major factors, the product's quality and the product's cost.

- It is important to remember that make or buy decisions affect both food and labor costs.

- Management, often in consultation with kitchen production staff, must resolve make or buy decisions.

- Generally, foodservice productivity ratios have not increased as have those of other businesses, since foodservice is a labor-intensive, rather than machine-intensive or technology-intensive industry.

- It is critical for the foodservice manager to understand the importance of a properly equipped workplace to improve productivity.

- Equipment should be properly maintained and updated if employees are to be held accountable for productivity standards or gains.

- Today's guest expects and demands higher levels of service than ever before, which require management to become creative in order to still improve employee productivity.

- When management varies service levels, it varies employee productivity ratios.

- The key to knowing "How many employees are needed?" to effectively operate the foodservice unit lies in developing productivity standards.

- The best productivity measure for any unit is, of course, the one that makes the most sense for that unique operation.

4. Measuring Current Labor Productivity

- There are a variety of ways to measure productivity in the hospitality industry. Commonly used measures of productivity include:
  - Labor cost percentage
  - Sales per labor hour
  - Labor dollars per guest served
  - Guests served per labor dollar
  - Guests served per labor hour
  - Revenue per available seat hour (RevPASH)

- The most commonly used measure of employee productivity in the foodservice industry is the **labor cost percentage**.

- The labor cost percentage is computed as follows:

$$\frac{\text{Cost of labor}}{\text{Total sales}} = \text{Labor cost \%}$$

- It is important to realize that managers may choose their own ways to define cost of labor when calculating their labor cost percentages.

- Controlling the labor cost percentage is extremely important in the foodservice industry, since it is the most widely used measure of worker productivity and thus is very often used to determine the effectiveness of a manager.

- Labor cost percentage varies with changes in the price paid for labor. Because of this, labor cost percentage by itself is not a complete measure of workforce productivity.

- The most perishable commodity any foodservice operator buys is the labor hour. When not productively used, it disappears forever. This is why many foodservice operators prefer to measure labor productivity in terms of the amount of sales generated for each labor hour used.

$$\frac{\text{Total sales}}{\text{Labor hours used}} = \text{Sales per labor hour}$$

- Sales per labor hour will vary with changes in menu selling price, but not with changes in the price paid for labor.

- However, sales per labor hour neglects to consider the amount paid to employees per hour to generate the sales. As a result, some managers prefer to measure productivity by calculating labor dollars per guest served.

$$\frac{\text{Cost of labor}}{\text{Guests served}} = \text{Labor dollars per guest served}$$

- With labor dollars per guest served, the cost of labor represents all the labor required to serve the guest.

- Labor dollars per guest served and guests served per labor dollar both vary based on the price paid for labor.

$$\frac{\text{Guests served}}{\text{Cost of labor}} = \text{Guests served per labor dollar}$$

- As a measure of productivity, guests served per labor dollar expended has advantages. It is relatively easy to compute, and can be used by foodservice units, such as institutions, that do not routinely record dollar sales figures.

- Guests served per labor hour is a powerful measure of productivity, not a measure of either cost and productivity or sales and productivity.

$$\frac{\text{Guests served}}{\text{Labor hours used}} = \text{Guests served per labor hour}$$

- Guests served per labor hour is extremely useful in comparing similar foodservice operations in areas with widely differing wage rates or selling prices. Managers who use this productivity tool do so because they like the focus of emphasizing service levels and not just reducing costs.

- While it is not a direct measure of labor productivity, **revenue per available seat hour (RevPASH)** helps managers evaluate how much guests buy and how quickly they are served. It does so primarily by assessing the duration and spending resulting from guests' dining experiences. Duration is simply the length of time customers sit at a table.

$$\frac{\text{Revenue}}{\text{Available seat hours}} = \text{Revenue per available seat hour (RevPASH)}$$

- Managers using the RevPASH ratio can gain valuable information about when their operations' labor needs are the greatest and then can use that information to efficiently schedule workers for each hour the operation is serving guests.

- Many operators prefer to compute their productivity measures on a daily, rather than on a weekly or monthly basis. This can easily be done by using a six-column form with cost of labor, sales, and labor cost percentage.

- Many operators find that a single measure of their labor productivity is insufficient for their needs—thus, they may use more than one measure.

- In addition, an operator may establish labor subcategories such as production, service, sanitation, and management.

- When determining labor productivity measures by subcategory, remember the following:
  - √ Be sure to include all the relevant data
  - √ Use the same method to identify the numerator and denominator for each category
  - √ Compute an overall total to ensure that the sum of the categories is consistent with the overall total.

- Labor costs for each subcategory can be estimated. By following the rules of algebra and adding the word *estimated,* the guests served per labor dollar formula can be restated as follows: Labor dollars per guest served and guests served per labor dollar both vary based on the price paid for labor.

$$\frac{\text{Number of estimated guests served}}{\text{Guests served per labor dollar}} = \text{Estimated cost of labor}$$

5. Managing Payroll Costs

- Essentially, the management of payroll costs is a four-step process, which includes the following factors:

    1. Determine productivity standards.
    2. Forecast sales volume.
    3. Schedule employees using productivity standards and forecasted sales volume.
    4. Analyze results.

- A **productivity standard** is defined as management's view of what constitutes an appropriate productivity ratio in a specific foodservice operation.

- Productivity standards represent what you should reasonably expect in the way of output per unit of labor input.

- Productivity standards are typically based on the following types of information: unit history, company average, industry average, management experience, or a combination of one or more of the above.

- A **franchisor** is the entity responsible for selling and maintaining control over the franchise brand's name.

- Sales volume forecasting, when combined with established labor productivity standards, allows a foodservice operator to determine the number of employees needed to effectively service your guests.

- You can establish a labor budget using your productivity standards, your sales forecast, and the labor cost percentage formula you have already learned. Remember that the labor cost percentage formula is defined as:

$$\frac{\text{Cost of labor}}{\text{Total sales}} = \text{Labor cost \%}$$

- If you include the words *forecasted, standard,* and *budget,* and follow the rules of algebra, the labor cost percentage formula can be restated as follows:

$$\text{Forecasted total sales} \times \text{Labor cost \% standard} = \text{Cost of labor budget}$$

- You can establish a budget for total number of labor hours needed to service your establishment. Remember, that guests served per labor hour formula is defined as:

$$\frac{\text{Guests served}}{\text{Labor hours used}} = \text{Guests served per labor hour}$$

- If you include the words *forecasted, standard,* and *budget,* and follow the rules of algebra, the guests served per labor hour formula can be restated as follows:

$$\frac{\text{Forecasted number of guests served}}{\text{Guests served per labor hours used}} = \text{Labor hour budget}$$

- Because employee schedules are based on the number of hours to be worked or dollars to be spent, an employee schedule recap form can be an effective tool in a daily analysis of labor productivity.

- Since labor is purchased on a daily basis, labor costs should be monitored on a daily basis.

- Some foodservice managers practice an **on-call** system whereby employees who are off duty are assigned to on-call status.

- Other managers practice a **call-in** system. In this arrangement, employees who are off duty are required to check in with management on a daily basis to see if the predicted sales volume is such that they may be needed.

- Schedule modifications should be done hourly, if necessary.

- It is critical to match scheduled labor usage with projected volume.

- To complete the job of managing labor-related expense, you should analyze your results by comparing your actual labor cost to your budgeted labor cost. To determine the percentage of budget, the following formula is used:

$$\frac{\text{Actual amount}}{\text{Budgeted amount}} = \% \text{ of budget}$$

- When referring to labor costs, some foodservice operators use the term *standard labor cost,* which is the labor cost needed to meet established productivity standards, rather than *budgeted cost.*

- In the case of labor, we may still be within reasonable budget, though we may vary greatly from the standard. For this reason, the authors prefer the term **budgeted labor** rather than **standard labor**. Labor standards will always vary a bit unless guest counts can be predicted perfectly, which is rarely the case.

- The complete process for establishing the labor schedule is summarized in the following 10-point checklist:

    1. Monitor historical operational data (or alternative data).
    2. Identify productivity standards.
    3. Forecast sales volume.
    4. Determine budgeted labor dollars or hours.
    5. Divide monthly budget into weekly budgets.
    6. Divide weekly budget into daily budgets.
    7. Segment daily budget into meal period budgets.
    8. Build schedule based on the budget.
    9. Analyze service levels during schedule period.
    10. Review and adjust productivity standards as needed.

6. Reducing Labor-Related Costs

- If management finds that labor costs are too high, problem areas must be identified and corrective action must be taken.

- Ways to reduce fixed labor costs include improving productivity, increasing sales volume, combining jobs to eliminate fixed positions, and reducing wages paid to the fixed payroll employees.

- Ways to reduce variable labor costs include; improving productivity, scheduling appropriately to adjust to changes in sales volume, combining jobs to eliminate variable positions, and reducing wages paid to the variable employees.

- One way to increase productivity and reduce labor-related expense is through **employee empowerment**, a process that consists of increasingly involving employees in the decision-making process.

- Today, employees have come to realize there is more to life than work. Management, unable to always offer more money, has been forced to come up with new incentives.

- Remember that most employees are seeking job satisfaction in addition to the salaries or wages paid to them.

7. Technology Tools

- As labor costs continue to increase, and as labor cost management becomes increasingly important to the profitability of restaurateurs, the tools available to manage these costs have increased significantly also.
- Current software programs can help you manage and control labor costs including the following tasks:

1. Maintain employment records such as:
   - Required employment documents (e.g., applications, I-9s and W-2s)
   - Tax data
   - Pay rates
   - Earned vacation or other leave time
   - Subcategories of labor data
   - Benefits eligibility
   - Training records

2. Conduct and record the results of online or computer-based training programs.
3. Compute voluntary and involuntary employee turnover rates by department.
4. Track employee lost days due to injury/accident.
5. Maintain employee availability records (requested days off, vacation, etc.).
6. Develop employee schedules and interface employee schedules with time clock systems.
7. Monitor overtime wages costs.
8. Maintain job descriptions and specifications.
9. Develop and maintain daily, weekly, and monthly productivity reports including:
   - Labor cost percentage
   - Sales per labor hour
   - Labor dollars per guest served
   - Guests served per labor dollar
   - Guests served per labor hour
   - Optimal labor costs based on actual sales achieved
10. Interface employee scheduling software with forecasted sales volume software in the POS system.

Key Terms & Concepts Review

Match the key terms with their correct definitions.

1. Payroll   _____

    a. The term used to designate the least number of employees, or payroll dollars, required to operate a facility or department within the facility.

2. Labor expense   _____

    b. A listing of the personal skills and characteristics needed to perform those tasks pertaining to a particular job description.

3. Salaried employee   _____

    c. The amount of work performed by a worker in a set amount of time.

4. Exempt employee   _____

    d. A system whereby employees who are off duty are required to check in with management on a daily basis to see if the volume is such that they may be needed.

5. Minimum staff   _____

    e. The labor cost needed to meet established productivity standards.

6. Fixed payroll   _____

    f. A method of training in which workers are training while they actually are performing their required tasks.

7. Variable payroll   _____

    g. Total wages and salaries paid by a business to its employees.

8. Productivity   _____

    h. Pre-employment tests such as typing tests for office employees, computer application tests for those involved in using word processing or spreadsheet tools, or food production tasks, as in the case of chefs.

9. Productivity ratio   _____

    i. The entity responsible for selling and maintaining control over the franchise name.

10. Job description   _____

    j. An employee who receives the same income per week or month regardless of the number of hours worked.

11. Job specification	_____	k.	A system whereby selected employees who are off duty can be contacted by management on short notice to cover for other employees who are absent or to come to work if customer demand suddenly increases.
12. Employment application	_____	l.	A pre-employment test used to determine if an applicant uses drugs. It is allowable in most states and can be a very effective tool for reducing insurance rates and potential employee liability issues.
13. Skills tests	_____	m.	A program usually held during the first week of an employee's job that provides information about important items such as dress code, disciplinary system, tip policy, lockers/security, sick leave policy, and retirement programs.
14. Psychological testing	_____	n.	The training undertaken to ensure an employee has the skills to meet productivity goals.
15. Pre-employment drug testing	_____	o.	Those dollars expended on employees whose presence is directly dependent on the number of guests served. These employees include servers, bartenders, and dishwashers, for example. As the number of guests served increases, the number of these individuals required to do the job also increases. As the number of guests served decreases, this should decrease.
16. Negligent hiring	_____	p.	Management causes the employee to separate from the organization (terminates the employee).
17. Orientation program	_____	q.	An event that describes employees who quit, are dismissed, or in some other manner have their employment with an operation terminated.
18. Task training	_____	r.	A scheduling technique used to match individual employee work shifts with the peaks and valleys of customer demand.

19. OJT	_____	s.	All expenses (costs), including payroll, required to maintain a workforce in a business.
20. On-the-floor	_____	t.	The amount of hourly income generated by each available seat in a foodservice operation.
21. Split-shift	_____	u.	Those dollars spent on employees, such as managers, receiving clerks, and dietitians, whose presence is not generally directly dependent on the number of guests served.
22. Employee separation	_____	v.	A calculation used to measure worker productivity. Total sales ÷ Labor hours used
23. Voluntary separation	_____	w.	A calculation used to measure worker productivity. Guests served ÷ Cost of labor
24. Involuntary separation	_____	x.	Salaried employee whose duties, responsibilities, and level of decisions make him or her "exempt" from the overtime provisions of the federal government's Fair Labor Standards Act (FLSA).
25. Labor cost percentage	_____	y.	An employee makes the decision to leave the organization.
26. Sales per labor hour	_____	z.	In the dining area.
27. Labor dollars per guest served	_____	aa.	Pre-employment testing that can include personality tests, tests designed to predict performance, or tests of mental ability.
28. Guests served per labor dollar	_____	bb.	Giving employees the power to make decisions.
29. Guests served per labor hour	_____	cc.	A calculation used to measure worker productivity. Cost of labor ÷ Total sales
30. Revenue per available seat hour (RevPASH)	_____	dd.	A formal document, completed by a candidate for employment, that lists the name, address, work experience, and related information of the candidate.
31. Productivity standard	_____	ee.	Failure on the part of an employer to exercise reasonable care in the selection of employees.

32. Franchisor	_____	ff.	This formula refers to the total unit output divided by the total unit input.
33. On-call	_____	gg.	Management's expectation of the productivity ratio of each employee. Also, management's view of what constitutes the appropriate productivity ratio in a given foodservice unit or units.
34. Call-in	_____	hh.	A calculation used to measure worker productivity. Guests served ÷ Cost of labor
35. Overtime wages	_____	ii.	A calculation used to measure worker productivity. Cost of labor ÷ Guests served
36. Standard labor cost	_____	jj.	A listing of the tasks to be performed in a particular position.
37. Empowerment	_____	kk.	Employee wages that, by law or policy, must be paid at a higher than normal rate.

Discussion Questions

1. List 10 key factors affecting employee productivity.

    _____
    _____
    _____
    _____

2. Identify and give the formulas used to calculate five different ways to measure productivity in the hospitality industry.

    _____
    _____
    _____
    _____

3. List and explain the importance of each of the four steps used to manage payroll costs.

    _____
    _____
    _____
    _____

4. List the approaches managers can utilize for reducing labor-related fixed expenses and labor-related variable expenses.

    _____
    _____
    _____
    _____

5. Explain how managers could combine information from a RevPASH analysis with their own targeted labor cost percentages to create effective employee schedules for dining room servers.

    _____
    _____
    _____
    _____

Quiz Yourself

Choose the letter of the best answer to the questions listed below.

1. Payroll is the term used to refer to the salaries and wages paid to employees.
   a. True
   b. False

2. Total labor expense in an operation will always be less than the operation's payroll.
   a. True
   b. False

3. Hourly paid employees are also referred to as exempt employees.
   a. True
   b. False

4. An operation's variable payroll is the amount that it pays to salaried workers.
   a. True
   b. False

5. Payroll is considered to be a controllable expense.
   a. True
   b. False

6. Productivity is the amount of work performed by an employee in a fixed period of time.
   a. True
   b. False

7. Input ÷ Output is the formula managers use to calculate a productivity ratio.
   a. True
   b. False

8. Managers can choose to use more than one type of formula when calculating their productivity ratios.
   a. True
   b. False

9. Productivity ratios help managers decide how much they should spend for payroll.
   a. True
   b. False

10. All foodservice operations can achieve the same levels of labor productivity.
    a. True
    b. False

11. What is the term for a listing of tasks that must be accomplished by an employee hired to fill a particular position in an operation?
    a. task analysis
    b. job description
    c. job specification
    d. empowerment checklist

12. A listing of the personal characteristics needed to perform the tasks required in a particular foodservice position is called a job
    a. analysis.
    b. description.
    c. explanation.
    d. specification.

13. Which is the first step that managers should take when developing an employee training program?
    a. Present the training
    b. Plan the training sessions
    c. Evaluate the training's effectiveness
    d. Determine how the task is to be done

14. Which formula calculates an operation's employee turnover rate?
    a. Number of employees separated × Number of employees in workforce
    b. Number of employees in workforce ÷ Number of employees separated
    c. Number of employees in workforce + Number of employees separated
    d. Number of employees separated ÷ Number of employees in workforce

15. Calculate the employee turnover rate using the following information: Number of employees separated = 45; Number of employees in workforce = 75.
    a. 1.7%
    b. 6.0%
    c. 17%
    d. 60%

16. "Make or buy" product decisions must consider product cost and
    a. staff reaction.
    b. product quality.
    c. product par levels.
    d. number of portions to be served.

Use the information below to answer Questions 17 through 21.

Operating Results for Brian's Caribbean Cafe

Sales Week	# of Guests Served	Labor Hours Used
1	12,000	8,100
2	11,280	7,200
3	10,320	6,400
4	13,200	10,600
Total	46,800	32,300
Average Guest Check	$18	
Average Wage per Hour	$7	
Total Sales	$842,400	
Total Labor Cost	$226,100	

17. What was Brian's labor cost percentage?
   a. 24.1%
   b. 26.8%
   c. 29.5%
   d. 32.3%

18. What were Brian's sales per labor hour used?
   a. $21.34
   b. $23.24
   c. $26.08
   d. $28.55

19. What was Brian's labor dollars per guest served?
   a. $4.83
   b. $5.53
   c. $6.75
   d. $7.15

20. What were Brian's guests served per labor dollar?
   a. 0.02
   b. 0.21
   c. 2.10
   d. 21.0

21. What were Brian's guests served per labor hour?
    a. 0.15
    b. 1.45
    c. 1.95
    d. 3.25

22. Which measure of labor productivity is not affected by changes in menu prices or changes in the cost paid for labor?
    a. sales per labor hour
    b. labor cost percentage
    c. guests served per labor hour
    d. labor dollars per guest served

23. To calculate RevPASH managers must know their operations' revenue, the number of seats available for sale, and the number of
    a. guests served.
    b. payroll dollars spent.
    c. hours the seats are available for use.
    d. minutes each guest remained in their seat.

24. What is the first step that managers must take to manage their payroll costs?
    a. Analyze results
    b. Forecast sales volume
    c. Determine productivity standards
    d. Schedule employees using sales forecasts and productivity standards

    Answer: c
    Difficulty: medium
    Section Reference: Managing Payroll Costs
    Learning Objective: Analyze and evaluate actual labor utilization

25. Who is the entity responsible for selling and maintaining control over a franchise brand's name?
    a. owner
    b. manager
    c. franchisor
    d. franchisee

26. Which formula will equal a manager's cost of labor budget?
    a. Forecasted total sales + Labor cost % standard
    b. Forecasted total sales × Labor cost % standard
    c. Forecasted total sales − Labor cost % standard
    d. Forecasted total sales ÷ Labor cost % standard

27. A manager forecasts she will serve 1500 guests. The manager's guest served per labor hour standard is 3.75 guests per hour. What should this manager's budgeted labor hours be?
    a. 250 hours
    b. 325 hours
    c. 400 hours
    d. 475 hours

28. How frequently must a manager monitor labor costs?
    a. daily
    b. weekly
    c. biweekly
    d. monthly

29. A manager budgeted $15,500 for labor. The manager actually spent $13,175 for labor. What percent of her labor budget did the manager spend?
    a. 65%
    b. 85%
    c. 98%
    d. 118%

30. If labor costs become too high, the best managers will
    a. take corrective action.
    b. reduce hourly pay rates.
    c. reduce employee salaries.
    d. terminate some employees.

31. What should be the impact on fixed cost percentage (FC%) and variable cost percentage (VC%) for labor when a professional manager increases his total sales?
    a. FC% increases and VC% increases
    b. FC% decreases and VC% decreases
    c. FC% increases and VC% is unchanged
    d. FC% decreases and VC% is unchanged

32. What should be the impact on variable cost (VC) for labor if a manager increases sales by attracting more guests to her foodservice operation?
    a. Total VC increases and VC% increases
    b. Total VC decreases and VC% decreases
    c. Total VC increases and VC% is unchanged
    d. Total VC decreases and VC% is unchanged

33. What would be the impact on fixed cost (FC) if the revenue in a manager's operation declines significantly?
    a. FC decreases and FC% increases
    b. FC decreases and FC% decreases
    c. FC is unchanged and FC% increases
    d. FC is unchanged and FC% decreases

34. Who has increased involvement in the decision-making process when an empowerment program is implemented in a foodservice operation?
    a. guests
    b. owners
    c. managers
    d. employees

Chapter Answers to Key Terms & Concepts Review, Discussion Questions, and Quiz Yourself

Key Terms & Concepts Review

1. g	7. o	13. h	19. f	25. cc	31. gg	37. bb
2. s	8. c	14. aa	20. z	26. v	32. i	
3. j	9. ff	15. l	21. r	27. ii	33. k	
4. x	10. jj	16. ee	22. q	28. w	34. d	
5. a	11. b	17. m	23. y	29. hh	35. kk	
6. u	12. dd	18. n	24. p	30. t	36. e	

Discussion Questions

1. List 10 key factors affecting employee productivity.
   - Employee selection
   - Training
   - Supervision
   - Scheduling
   - Breaks
   - Morale
   - Menu
   - Convenience versus scratch preparation
   - Equipment
   - Service level desired

2. Identify and give the formulas used to calculate five different ways to measure productivity in the hospitality industry.
   - Labor cost percentage: The cost of labor includes payroll and total labor costs.

     Formula:
     $$\text{Labor cost percentage} = \text{Cost of labor} \div \text{Total sales}$$
   - Sales per labor hour: The most perishable commodity any foodservice operator buys is the labor hour. When it is not productively used, it disappears forever.

     Formula:
     $$\text{Sales per labor hour} = \text{Total sales} \div \text{Labor hours used}$$

- Labor dollars per guest served: This measure varies based on the price paid for labor.

  Formula:

  Labor dollars per guest served = Cost of labor ÷ Guests served

- Guests served per labor dollar: This tool includes all the labor cost required to serve an operation's guests.

  Formula:

  Guests served per labor dollar = Guests served ÷ Cost of labor

- Guest served per labor hour: This is a true measure of productivity, not a measure of either cost and productivity or sales and productivity. It is extremely useful in comparing similar units in areas with widely differing wage rates or selling prices.

  Formula:

  Guests served per labor hour = Guests served ÷ Labor hours used

- Revenue Per Available Seat Hour (RevPASH): This is an indirect measure of an operation's ability to process guests efficiently.

  Formula:

  RevPASH = Revenue ÷ Available seat hours

3. List and explain the importance of each of the four steps used to manage payroll costs.
   - Step 1. Determine productivity standards: Managers must first determine the productivity standards they will used to assess their operations. This may be a single measurement, such as labor cost percentage, or any other of a number of alternative productivity measures.
   - Step 2. Forecast sales volume: Managers forecast sales volume to estimate the number of guests that must be served in the future and the amount of food and beverage products that will likely need to be produced.
   - Step 3. Schedule employees using productivity standards and forecasted sales volume. When productivity standards are known in sales forecasts are created managers can produce employee schedules designed to achieve the productivity standard to properly serve guests.
   - Step 4. Analyze results: Managers analyze their labor productivity results to identify areas in which improvements can be made.

4. List the approaches managers can utilize for reducing labor-related fixed expenses and labor-related variable expenses.
   - Reducing labor-related fixed expenses
     - Improve productivity
     - Increase sale volume
     - Combine jobs to eliminate fixed positions
     - Reduce wages paid to the fixed-payroll employees
   - Reducing labor-related variable expenses
     - Improve productivity
     - Schedule appropriately to adjust to changes in sales volume
     - Combine jobs to eliminate variable positions
     - Reduce wages paid to the variable employees

5. Explain how managers could combine information from a RevPASH analysis with their own targeted labor cost percentages to create effective employee schedules for dining room servers.
   - The results of a RevPASH analysis tells managers when they are generating the most revenue in their dining areas. Managers can use this information to schedule workers at peak demand times. For example, if a manager knows revenue during a specific time period will be $1,000, and the manager's targeted labor cost is 35 percent, then $350 in labor dollars can be expended during this time period.

Quiz Yourself

1. a.	10. b.	19. a.	28. a.
2. b.	11. b.	20. b.	29. b.
3. b.	12. d.	21. b.	30. a.
4. b.	13. d.	22. b.	31. d.
5. a.	14. d.	23. c.	32. c.
6. a.	15. d.	24. c.	33. c.
7. b.	16. b.	25. c.	34. d.
8. a.	17. b.	26. b.	
9. a.	18. c.	27. b.	

Chapter 8

Controlling Other Expenses

Learning Outcomes

At the conclusion of this chapter, you will be able to:

- Classify other expenses as being either controllable or non-controllable.

  In addition to the food, beverage, and labor expense managers incur when operating their units, there are "other" operating expenses that must be paid. These other expenses can account for a significant amount of the total cost of operating a foodservice unit.

  Some of these other expenses are directly under the control of management. When following the USAR, these types of expense are reported on an operation's income statement as "Other controllable expenses." Some other expenses are not directly controllable by management and these are reported on the income statement as "Non-controllable expenses." Because managers should spend their time addressing controllable rather than non-controllable expenses, it is important that you be able to classify other expenses as being either controllable or non-controllable.

- Categorize other expenses in terms of being fixed, variable, or mixed.

  Operating costs can be classified as either controllable or non-controllable but, in addition, all costs can also be categorized as being fixed, variable, or mixed.

  If a manager is to properly analyze other expenses they incur he or she must be able to categorize other expenses as being fixed, variable, or mixed to better assess whether these costs are being properly managed.

- Compute other expense costs in terms of cost per guest and as a percentage of sales.

  In the hospitality industry food, beverage and labor costs are commonly reported in whole dollar amounts and as a percentage of sales. In a similar manner, other expenses required to operate a foodservice facility are also reported in terms of their dollar amount and their percentage of total revenue.

  If managers are to successfully control their other operating expenses, they must be able to assess those expenses by reviewing the total amount of the expense and the total amount as a proportion of the sales the costs helped to generate.

Study Notes

1. Other Expenses

- **Other expenses** are those cost items that are neither food, beverage, nor labor.

- Other expenses can account for a significant amount of the total cost of operating your foodservice unit.

- You must look for ways to control all of your expenses, but sometimes the environment in which you operate will act upon your facility to influence some of your costs in positive or negative ways.

- For example, in the past, serving water to each guest upon arrival in a restaurant was simply **SOP** (standard operating procedure) for many operations. The rising cost of energy and increased awareness on the environment of wasted resources has caused many foodservice operations to implement a policy of serving water on request rather than with each order.

- Energy conservation and waste recycling are two examples of attempts to control and reduce other expenses.

2. Controllable and Non-controllable Other Expenses

- Each foodservice operation will have its own unique list of required other expenses.

- An other expense can constitute almost any cost incurred in the foodservice business.

- If cost groupings are used, they should make sense to the operator and should be specific enough to let the operator know what is in the category.

- Operators can use their own categories, or follow those used in the *Uniform System of Accounts for Restaurants* (*USAR*).

- Although some operators may prefer to make up their own other expense cost categories, the cost categories generally recommended by the USAR are divided into two primary groups:
    - Other Controllable Expenses
    - Non-controllable Expenses

- A **controllable expense** is one in which decisions made by the foodservice manager can have the direct effect of either increasing or reducing the expense.

- A **non-controllable expense** is one in which most actions by the foodservice manager can neither increase nor decrease the expense.

- Within the two primary *USAR* expense groups, recommended sub-groupings for individual cost categories are:

    1. Other Controllable Expenses
        - Direct Operating Expenses
        - Music and Entertainment
        - Marketing
        - Utilities
        - General and Administrative Expenses
        - Repairs and Maintenance

    2. Non-controllable Expenses
        - Occupancy Costs
        - Equipment Rental
        - Depreciation and Amortization
        - Corporate Overhead (multiunit restaurants)
        - Management Fees
        - Interest Expense

- Within each other expense cost sub-grouping, an operation's individual other expenses may be even further detailed to aid managers in their reporting and decision-making.

- In most cases, managers should focus their attention on controllable rather than non-controllable expenses.

3. Fixed, Variable, and Mixed Other Expenses

- As an effective cost control manager, it is important to recognize the difference between expenses that are fixed and those expenses that vary as revenue varies.

- A **fixed expense** is one that remains constant despite increases or decreases in sales volume.

- A **variable expense** is one that generally increases as sales volume increases, and decreases as sales volume decreases.

- A **mixed expense** is one that has properties of both a fixed and a variable expense.

- The following shows how fixed, variable, and mixed expenses are affected as sales volume increases:

159

Expense	As a Percentage of Sales	Total Dollars
Fixed Expense	Decreases	Remains the same
Variable Expense	Remains the same	Increases
Mixed Expense	Decreases	Increases

- If an operator feels that a fixed expense percentage is too high, he or she must either increase sales or negotiate lower costs to reduce the cost percentage.

- Normal variations in expense percentage that relate *only* to whether an expense is fixed, variable, or mixed should not be of undue concern to management. It is only when a fixed expense is too high or a variable expense is out of control that management should act. This is called the concept of **management by exception.**

4. Monitoring Other Expenses

- When managing other expenses, two control and monitoring alternatives are available:

    1. Other expense cost percentage
    2. Other expense cost per guest

$$\frac{\text{Other expense}}{\text{Total sales}} = \text{Other expense cost \%}$$

$$\frac{\text{Other expenses}}{\text{Number of guests served}} = \text{Other expense costs per guest}$$

- The other expense cost per guest formula is of particular value when management believes it can be helpful, or when lack of a daily or monthly sales figure makes the computation of other expense cost percentage impossible.
- Increasingly, foodservice managers are finding that creative "Green" initiatives benefit their operations in many ways, including those that reduce other expenses. "Trayless dining" is just such an example.

- Trayless operations experience a 30–50 percent reduction in food and beverage waste. Diners take less food (because they only want to carry what they know they will eat). Without trays to wash, water consumption is also decreased. The result is a decrease in other expenses such as water, utilities, and cleaning products.

5. Managing Other Expenses

- To reduce costs, it is useful to break down other expenses into four main categories: food and beverage, labor, facility maintenance, and occupancy when developing strategies for lower overall other expense costs.

- In general, fixed costs related to food and beverage operations can only be reduced when measuring them as a percentage of total sales. This can be done only by increasing an operation's total sales generated.

- Labor-related expenses can generally be considered partially fixed and partially variable.

- To reduce costs related to labor, it is necessary to eliminate wasteful labor-related expense. However, if an operator attempts to reduce other expenses related to labor too much, he or she may find that the best workers prefer to work elsewhere.

- Reducing employee benefits while attempting to retain a well-qualified workforce is, in most cases, an ineffective strategy.

- A properly designed and implemented preventative maintenance program can go a long way toward reducing equipment failure and thus decreasing equipment and facility-related costs.

- Proper care of mechanical equipment prolongs its life and reduces operational costs.

- One way to help ensure that costs are as low as possible is to use a competitive bid process before awarding contracts for services you require.

- In the area of maintenance contracts, for areas such as the kitchen or for mechanical equipment, elevators, or grounds, it is recommended that these contracts be bid at least once per year.

- Air-conditioning, plumbing, heating, and refrigerated units should be inspected at least yearly, and kitchen equipment should be inspected at least monthly for purposes of preventative maintenance.

- **Occupancy costs** refer to those expenses incurred by the foodservice unit that are related to the occupancy of and payment for the physical facility it occupies.

- For the foodservice manager who is not the owner, the majority of occupancy costs will be non-controllable. Rent, mortgages, taxes, and interest on debt are real costs but are most often beyond the immediate control of the unit manager.

- Total controllable and non-controllable other expenses in an operation can range from 5 to 15 percent or even more of the unit's total sales.

6. Technology Tools

- Depending on the specific foodservice operation, other expenses can represent a significant portion of the operations total operating costs. As a result, controlling these costs is just as important as controlling food and labor-related costs.

- Software and hardware that can be purchased to assist in this area include applications that relate to:

  1. Assessing and monitoring utilities cost
  2. Minimizing energy costs via the use of motion-activated sensors
  3. Managing equipment maintenance records
  4. Tracking marketing costs/benefits
  5. Menu and promotional materials printing hardware and software
  6. Analysis of communications costs (telephone tolls websites and social media)
  7. Analysis of all other expense costs on a "cost per-guest" basis
  8. Analysis of all other expense costs on a "cost per dollar sale" basis
  9. Comparing building/contents insurance costs across alternative insurance providers
  10. Software programs designed to assist in the preparation of the income statement, balance sheet, and the statement of cash flows
  11. Income tax management
  12. Income tax filing

- At the minimum, most independent operators should computerize their records related to taxes at all levels to ensure accuracy, safekeeping, and timeliness of required filings.

Key Terms & Concepts Review

Match the key terms with their correct definitions.

1. Other controllable expenses _____

   a. Term used for the way something is done in normal business operations.

2. Non-controllable expenses _____

   b. An expense that has properties of both a fixed and a variable expense.

3. Standard operating procedure (SOP) _____

   c. An expense that generally increases as sales volume increases and decreases as sales volume decreases.

4. Fixed expense _____

   d. The measure of electrical usage.

5. Variable expense _____

   e. An expense that the foodservice manager can neither increase nor decrease.

6. Mixed expense _____

   f. Nonfood and beverage costs that can be directly influenced by management action. Examples include advertising expense, utility costs, and the costs of repair and maintenance of equipment.

7. Management by exception _____

   g. Heating, ventilation, and air-conditioning.

8. Kilowatt-hour (kWh) _____

   h. Expenses related to occupying and paying for the physical facility that houses the foodservice unit.

9. Heating, ventilation, and air-conditioning (HVAC) _____

   i. If an expense is within an acceptable variation range, there is no need for management to intervene. Management takes corrective action only when operational results are outside the range of acceptability.

10. Occupancy costs _____

   j. An expense that remains constant despite increases or decreases in sales volume.

Discussion Questions

1. Identify the three different types of expenses and the impact on each resulting from increases or decreases in sales volume.

Expense	Impact of Increased Sales on		Impact of Decreased Sales on	
Type	% of Sales	Total $	% of Sales	Total $

2. List four areas in which hospitality managers can reduce other expenses.

_____

_____

_____

_____

3. Define and give examples of controllable and non-controllable other expenses.

_____

_____

_____

_____

4. Identify two formulas for controlling and monitoring other expenses.

_____

_____

_____

_____

5. What impacts will an operation's decision to implement green initiatives likely have on the operation's other expense costs? Provide examples to support your answer.

_____

_____

_____

_____

Quiz Yourself

1. Other expenses in a foodservice operation will include the cost of mandated payroll taxes.
    a. True
    b. False

2. Waste recycling is an example of an effort to reduce an operation's other expense costs.
    a. True
    b. False

3. Controlling portion size is an example of an effort to reduce an operation's other expense costs.
    a. True
    b. False

4. All foodservice operations will encounter the same other expense costs.
    a. True
    b. False

5. The *Uniform System of Accounts for Restaurants* (*USAR*) lists suggested cost groupings for a foodservice operation's other expenses.
    a. True
    b. False

6. How many primary cost categories does the USAR recommend managers use to organize their other expense costs?
    a. 1
    b. 2
    c. 3
    d. 4

7. Which type of expense can be most easily influenced by the actions of a foodservice manager?
    a. fixed
    b. occupancy
    c. controllable
    d. non-controllable

8. Which type of expense will be least influenced by the actions of a foodservice manager?
    a. fixed
    b. occupancy
    c. controllable
    d. non-controllable

9. Which operating cost would normally be classified under the "Other Controllable Expenses" category?
   a. rent
   b. utilities
   c. interest expense
   d. management fees

10. Which operating cost would normally be classified under the "Non-Controllable Expenses" category?
    a. utilities
    b. marketing
    c. equipment rental
    d. repairs and maintenance

11. When sales volume in an operation increases, the operation's fixed expenses
    a. will increase.
    b. will decrease.
    c. will stay the same.
    d. could increase or decrease.

12. Which is an example of a variable expense in a foodservice operation?
    a. license fees
    b. napkin expense
    c. mortgage interest
    d. equipment rental expense

13. A manager pays a monthly fee for extermination services. What will be the effect on total dollars spent and dollars spent as a percentage of sales for extermination costs if the operation's sales increase by 10 percent this month compared to last month?
    a. Total dollars spent will increase and the expense percentage will increase
    b. Total dollars spent will increase and the expense percentage will decrease
    c. Total dollars spent will be unchanged and the expense percentage will increase
    d. Total dollars spent will be unchanged and the expense percentage will decrease

14. An operation pays an outside valet service company a per-car rate for parking its customers cars. What should be the effect on total dollars spent and dollars spent as a percentage of sales for valet parking costs if the operation's sales increase by 10 percent this month compared to last month?
    a. Total dollars spent will increase and the expense percentage will increase
    b. Total dollars spent will decrease and the expense percentage will decrease
    c. Total dollars spent will increase and the expense percentage will stay the same
    d. Total dollars spent will decrease and the expense percentage will stay the same

15. The "management by exception" concept requires managers to act when
    a. menu prices rise excessively.
    b. customer counts rise considerably.
    c. a variable expense percentage rises dramatically.
    d. fixed expense as a percentage of sales declines significantly.

16. What type of expense changes in direct proportion to increases or decreases in an operation's revenue?
    a. fixed
    b. variable
    c. controllable
    d. non-controllable

Haley has kept records of the costs and sales volume achieved for the last four bands she booked at her jazz club. Use her information below to answer Questions 17 through 21.

Unit Name: Haley's Jazz Club

Date	Band	Band Expense	Club Sales	Cost %	# of Guests Served	Cost per Guest Served
01/15	The Chick-a-Dees	$8,000	$41,000		4,217	
02/15	Bakers Boys	$5,500	$30,000		3,800	
03/15	The Staples	$6,500	$33,000		4,000	
04/15	Guitar Heroes	$3,000	$20,000		2,500	

17. What was the Band Cost % for the Chick-a-Dees?
    a. 9.2
    b. 12.3
    c. 19.5
    d. 26.1

18. What was the cost per guest served for the Chick-a-Dees?
    a. $1.83
    b. $2.02
    c. $1.90
    d. $1.63

19. Which band had the highest cost per guest served?
    a. The Staples
    b. Baker's Boys
    c. Guitar Heroes
    d. The Chick-a-Dees

20. Which band should Haley choose if she wanted to rebook the one providing the lowest cost per guest served?
    a. The Staples
    b. Baker's Boys
    c. Guitar Heroes
    d. The Chick-a-Dees

21. Which band should Haley choose if she wanted to rebook the one providing the lowest Band Cost %?
    a. The Staples
    b. Baker's Boys
    c. Guitar Heroes
    d. The Chick-a-Dees

22. An operation's other expense cost percentage is equal to the operation's
    a. Total sales × Total expenses.
    b. Other expenses ÷ Total sales.
    c. Other expenses × Total sales.
    d. Total sales ÷ Other expenses.

23. A manager's operation achieved $100,000 in sales last year. What amount did this manager's operation likely pay for "other expenses" last year?
    a. Less than $50,000
    b. $50,000 – $150,000
    c. $250,000 – $350,000
    d. $450,000 – $550,000

24. How can the manager of a beverage operation reduce a fixed other expense cost percentage?
    a. increase sales
    b. reduce labor costs
    c. reduce occupancy costs
    d. increase drink portion sizes

25. Calculate an operation's other expense cost percentage for advertising using the following information: Advertising expense = $4,500; Number of guests served = 10,000; Total sales = $95,000.
    a. 4.5%
    b. 4.7%
    c. 47%
    d. 45%

26. A manager in a shopping mall food court must pay 8 percent of sales for rent. Last month, the managers sales were $66,000. How much rent did the manager pay last month?
    a. $528
    b. $1,212
    c. $5,280
    d. $12,121

27. A manager pays $10,000 per month plus 3 percent of total monthly sales to the owner of the building that houses the manager's restaurant. How much will the manager have to pay the landlord in a month in which her operation's total sales were $180,000?
    a. $15,400
    b. $20,400
    c. $25,400
    d. $30,400

28. A person pays $5,000 per month plus 8 percent of total monthly sales to lease his own food cart in a busy downtown area. How much must be paid to the cart's owner in a month in which total monthly sales were $36,000?
    a. $5,000
    b. $7,880
    c. $8,000
    d. $10,880

29. A manager of a nightclub pays $1,000 per year for a dance permit required by state law. Which type of other expense should the manager consider this cost to be?
    a. controllable, fixed
    b. controllable, variable
    c. non-controllable, fixed
    d. non-controllable, variable

30. How many times per year should managers accept bids for the maintenance of their major equipment such as HVAC system?
    a. one time
    b. two times
    c. three times
    d. four times

31. Which expense would be considered an occupation cost?
    a. labor
    b. utilities
    c. equipment repair
    d. mortgage payment

32. Who most influences the amount an operation will pay for occupancy costs?
    a. owners
    b. managers
    c. employees
    d. franchisors

Chapter Answers to Key Terms & Concepts Review, Discussion Questions, and Quiz Yourself

Key Terms & Concepts Review

1. f	6. b
2. e.	7. i
3. a	8. d
4. j	9. g
5. c	10. h

Discussion Questions

1. Identify the three different types of expenses and the effect on each of them resulting from increases and decreases in sales volume.

Expense	Impact of Increased Sales on		Impact of Decreased Sales on	
Type	% of Sales	Total $	% of Sales	Total $
Fixed	Decreases	Remains the same	Increases	Remains the same
Variable	Remains the same	Increases	Remains the same	Decreases
Mixed	Decreases	Increases	Increases	Decreases

2. List four areas in which hospitality managers can reduce other expenses.
   - Reducing costs related to food and beverage operations
   - Reducing costs related to labor
   - Reducing costs related to facility maintenance
   - Reducing occupancy costs

3. Define and give examples of controllable and non-controllable other expenses.
   - Controllable expense: Expenses for which decisions made by the foodservice manager can have the effect of either increasing or reducing the expense.

     Examples of controllable expenses include:
     - Uniforms
     - Rented equipment
     - Marketing
     - Live music expense
     - Utilities

   - Non-controllable expense: Expenses that a foodservice manager can neither increase nor decrease.

Examples of non-controllable expenses include:

>> Depreciation
>> Insurance premiums
>> Rent
>> Licenses
>> Interest on loans

4. Identify two formulas for controlling and monitoring other expenses.
   - Other expense cost %
   Formula:
   > Other expense cost % = Other expense ÷ Total sales

   - Other expense cost per guest
   Formula:
   > Other expense cost per guest = Other expense ÷ Number of guests served

5. What impacts will an operation's decision to implement green initiatives likely have on the operation's other expense costs? Provide examples to support your answer.
   - In most cases, a foodservice operator's decision to implement green initiatives will reduce other expense costs. For example, efforts to reduce the use of water will result in lowered water costs. Efforts to reduce electrical consumption will reduce consumption and thus lower utility bills. Efforts to implement source reduction in cooperation with vendors may result in reduced waste disposal costs.
   - In some cases, a green initiative requires an initial investment on the part of an operation. For example, replacing inefficient light bulbs with more efficient bulbs may cause the operation to incur immediate cost. Those cost can be recovered over time, however, because the more efficient light bulbs generate lower utility usage and thus will lower future utility bills.

Quiz Yourself

1. b.	9. b.	17. c.	25. b.
2. a.	10. c.	18. c.	26. b.
3. b.	11. c.	19. d.	27. a.
4. b.	12. b.	20. c.	28. b.
5. a.	13. d.	21. c.	29. a.
6. b.	14. c.	22. b.	30. a.
7. c.	15. c.	23. b.	31. d.
8. d.	16. b.	24. a.	32. a.

Chapter 9

Analyzing Results Using the Income Statement

Learning Outcomes

At the conclusion of this chapter, you will be able to:

- Prepare an income (P&L) statement.

    The income statement is the financial report that details the sales achieved, the money spent on expenses, and the resulting profit generated by a business during a specific time period. Its formal title is the "Statement of Income and Expense," but it is popularly referred to as the income statement, the profit and loss statement, or the P&L.

    Because the income statement provides a financial summary of a business's operations, it is essential that managers be able to prepare a P&L in a manner that is consistent with accepted accounting procedures. When they can, the information on their P&Ls can be read and understood by those managers, companies, owners, investors, and others interested in knowing about the financial performance of the operation.

- Analyze sales and expenses using the income statement.

    The analysis of an income statement is a creative process. Knowledgeable managers can learn much about their operations from a thoughtful assessment of the information presented in an income statement.

    When managers can properly analyze the sales and expenses of their operations using an income statement, they will gain a greater understanding of their operations' revenue, food expense, beverage expense, labor expense, other expenses, and resulting profits.

- Evaluate a facility's profitability using the income statement.

    Most businesses are operated for the purpose of generating a profit. Even nonprofit operations must generate more revenue than expense in order to maintain themselves over a long period of time. As a result, managers' abilities to assess the profitability of their own, and other, businesses is an essential skill that all professionals in the foodservice industry must acquire.

Study Notes

1. Introduction to Financial Analysis

- Foodservice managers, more often than not, find themselves awash in numbers! This information, in an appropriate form, is necessary not only to effectively operate your business but also to serve many interest groups that are directly or indirectly involved with the financial operation of your facility.

- When operating a business, managers should want to know:

  ✓ How much money did we take in?
  ✓ How much money did we spend?
  ✓ How much profit did we make?

- Documenting and analyzing sales, expenses, and profits is sometimes called **cost accounting,** but more appropriately it is known as **managerial accounting** to reflect the importance managers place on this process.

- It is important for you to know the difference between **bookkeeping**, the process of simply recording and summarizing financial data, and the actual analysis of that data.

- While bookkeeping is only the summarizing and recording of data, managerial accounting involves the summarizing, recording, and most importantly, the analysis of data.

- Managers do not need to be a **certified management accountant (CMA)** or a **certified public accountant (CPA)** to analyze data related to foodservice revenue and expense.

- In 2002, the United States Congress passed the **Sarbanes–Oxley Act (SOX)**. Technically known as the Public Company Accounting Reform and Investor Protection Act, the law provides criminal penalties for those found to have committed accounting fraud.

2. Uniform Systems of Accounts

- Financial reports related to the operation of a foodservice facility are of interest to management, stockholders, owners, creditors, governmental agencies, and, often, the general public.

- To ensure that this financial information is presented in a way that is both useful and consistent, **uniform systems of accounts** have been established for many areas of the hospitality industry.

174

- The National Restaurant Association has developed *the Uniform System of Accounts for Restaurants* (USAR). The *USAR* seeks to provide a consistent and clear manner in which foodservice managers can record sales, expenses, and the overall financial condition of their operating units.

- The uniform systems of accounts are guidelines, not a mandated methodology. Small foodservice operations, for example, may use the *USAR* in a slightly different way than will large operations.

3. Income Statement (*USAR* format)

- The **income statement** is often referred to as the profit and loss (P&L) statement, and is a summary report that describes the sales achieved, the money spent on expenses and the resulting profit generated by a business in a specific time period.

- A purpose of the **profit and loss statement** is to identify **net income**, which is the profit generated after all appropriate expenses of a business have been paid.

- Each operation's P&L statement may look slightly different.

- A precise definition of exactly what is meant by the term *profit* must be established for each P&L statement if it is to be helpful and communicate information accurately.

- The *USAR* can best be understood by evaluating its four major sections:
    1. Sales
    2. Prime costs
    3. Other controllable costs
    4. Non-Controllable expenses

- These four sections are arranged on the income statement *from most controllable to least controllable* by the foodservice manager (see sample income statement below).

Sample Income Statement (Figure 9.1 from Chapter 9)					
Joshua's Inc.					
	Last Year	%		This Year	%
SALES					
Food	$1,891,011	82.0%		$2,058,376	81.0%
Beverage	415,099	18.0%		482,830	19.0%
Total Sales	**$2,306,110**	**100.0%**		**$2,541,206**	**100.0%**
COST OF SALES					
Food	$ 712,587	37.7%		$ 767,443	37.3%
Beverages	94,550	22.8%		96,566	20.0%
Total Cost of Sales	**$ 807,137**	**35.0%**		**$ 864,009**	**34.0%**
LABOR					
Management	$ 128,219	5.6%		$ 142,814	5.6%
Staff	512,880	22.2%		571,265	22.5%
Employee Benefits	99,163	4.3%		111,813	4.4%
Total Labor	**$ 740,262**	**32.1%**		**$ 825,892**	**32.5%**
PRIME COST	**$1,547,399**	**67.1%**		**$1,689,901**	**66.5%**
OTHER CONTROLLABLE EXPENSES					
Direct Operating Expenses	$ 122,224	5.3%		$ 132,143	5.2%
Music & Entertainment	2,306	0.1%		7,624	0.3%
Marketing	43,816	1.9%		63,530	2.5%
Utilities	73,796	3.2%		88,942	3.5%
General & Administrative Expenses	66,877	2.9%		71,154	2.8%
Repairs & Maintenance	34,592	1.5%		35,577	1.4%
Total Other Controllable Expenses	**$ 343,611**	**14.9%**		**$ 398,970**	**15.7%**
CONTROLLABLE INCOME	**$ 415,100**	**18.0%**		**$ 452,335**	**17.8%**
NON-CONTROLLABLE EXPENSES					
Occupancy Costs	$ 120,000	5.2%		$ 120,000	4.7%
Equipment Leases	–	0.0%		–	0.0%
Depreciation & Amortization	41,510	1.8%		55,907	2.2%
Total Non-Controllable Expenses	161,510	7.0%		175,907	6.9%
RESTAURANT OPERATING INCOME	**$ 253,590**	**11.0%**		**$ 276,428**	**10.9%**
Interest Expense	86,750	3.8%		84,889	3.3%
INCOME BEFORE INCOME TAXES	**$ 166,840**	**7.2%**		**$ 191,539**	**7.5%**
Income Taxes	65,068	2.8%		76,616	3.0%
NET INCOME	**$ 101,772**	**4.4%**		**$ 114,923**	**4.5%**

Note 1: Income Statement format is based on the USAR, 8th ed., with the inclusion of income taxes and net income.
Note 2: All percentages are computed as a percentage of Total Sales except Cost of Sales line items, which are based on their respective category sales.

- Sales simply refers to the revenue generated by a business in the accounting period for which the income statement was prepared.

- **Prime cost** is defined as an operation's total cost of sales added to its total labor cost. Prime cost is clearly listed on the P&L because it is an excellent indicator of management's ability to control the costs of sales and labor—the two largest expenses in most foodservice operations.

- **Other controllable costs** are those nonfood, nonbeverage, and nonlabor costs controlled by the manager, but more so on a weekly or monthly basis (with the exception of employee wages, which you can most often control daily).

- The **Non-controllable expenses** section lists those costs that are least controllable by the foodservice manager. For example, interest paid to creditors as part of short-term or long-term debt repayment is due regardless of the ability of the manager to control day-to-day operating costs.

- Managers most often choose **restaurant operating income** (the operating income subtotal before interest expense is subtracted) or **income before income taxes** (the operating income after interest expense is subtracted, but before income taxes are subtracted) as the most relevant indicators of management performance. This is because most managers do not have control over interest expense paid or the taxes due on profits that have been generated by a business.

- On a P&L, each revenue and expense category is expressed both in terms of its whole dollar amount and its percentage of total sales. All ratios are calculated as a percentage of total sales except the following:
    - Food costs are divided by food sales.
    - Beverage costs are divided by beverage sales.

- The income statement is an **aggregate statement**. This means that all details associated with the sales, cost, and profits of the foodservice establishment are *summarized* on the P&L statement. Although this summary gives the manager a look at the overall performance of the operation, details of income and expense are not included directly on the statement.

- These details can be found in **supporting schedules**. Each line item on the income statement should be accompanied by a schedule that outlines all of the information that you, as a manager, need to know to operate your business successfully.

Sample Supporting Schedule (Figure 9.2 from Chapter 9)

Direct Operating Expenses Schedule

Type of Expense	Expense	% of Direct Operating Expenses	Notes
Uniforms	$ 13,408	10.15%	
Laundry and Linen	40,964	31.00%	
China and Glassware	22,475	17.01%	Expense is higher than budgeted because china shelf collapsed on March 22.
Silverware	3,854	2.92%	
Kitchen Utensils	9,150	6.92%	
Linen	2,542	1.92%	
Cleaning Supplies	10,571	8.00%	
Paper Supplies	2,675	2.02%	
Bar Uniforms	5,413	4.10%	
Menus and Wine Lists	6,670	5.05%	Expense is lower than budgeted because the new wine supplier agreed to print the wine lists free of charge.
Exterminating	1,803	1.36%	
Flowers and Decorations	9,014	6.82%	
Licenses	3,604	2.73%	
Total Direct Operating Expenses	$132,143	100.00%	

- It is in the supporting schedules that you will collect the information you need to break down sales or costs in detail and thus determine problem areas and potential opportunities for improving each item on the income statement.

- The P&L statement is one of several documents that can help evaluate the financial health of a business. In general, managers who seek to discover all that their P&L will tell them undertake the following areas of analysis.

      1. Sales/volume
      2. Food expense
      3. Beverage expense
      4. Labor expense
      5. Other controllable and non-controllable expense
      6. Profits

4. Analysis of Sales/Volume

- Foodservice operators can measure sales in terms of either dollars or number of guests served. A sales increase or decrease must, however, be analyzed carefully if you are to truly understand the revenue direction of your business.

- Overall sales increases or decreases can be computed using the following steps:

  1. Determine sales for this accounting period.
  2. Calculate the following: this period's sales minus last period's sales.
  3. Divide the difference in step 2 by last period's sales to determine percentage variance.

- There are several ways a foodservice operation experiences total sales volume increases:

  1. Serve the same number of guests at a higher check average.
  2. Serve more guests at the same check average.
  3. Serve more guests at a higher check average.
  4. Serve *fewer* guests at a *much* higher check average.

- The procedure to adjust sales variance to include known menu price increases is as follows:

  Step 1. Increase prior-period sales (last year) by amount of the price increase.
  Step 2. Subtract the result in Step 1 from this period's sales.
  Step 3. Divide the difference in Step 2 by the value of Step 1.

- Every critical factor must be considered when evaluating sales revenue, including the number of operating meal periods or days; changes in menu prices, guest counts, and check averages; and special events.

5. Analysis of Food Expense

- For the effective foodservice manager, the analysis of food expense is a matter of major concern.

- It is important to remember that the numerator of the food cost percentage equation is cost of food sold, while the denominator is total food sales, rather than total food and beverage sales.

- A food cost percentage can be computed for each food subcategory. For instance, the cost percentage for a category created for Meats and Seafood would be computed as follows:

$$\frac{\text{Meats and seafood costs}}{\text{Total food sales}} = \text{Meats and seafood cost \%}$$

- Many operators feel **gross profit** is a key number because it assesses food and beverage sales, and those food and beverage-related costs that can and should be directly controlled by the manager on a daily basis.

$$\text{Total sales} - \text{Total cost of sales} = \text{Gross profit}$$

- Earlier editions of the *USAR* actually included gross profit calculations, but the most recent edition does not. In many other countries, however, gross profit remains a key entry on the income statement.

- **Inventory turnover** refers to the number of times the total value of inventory has been purchased and replaced in an accounting period.

- The formula used to compute inventory turnover is:

$$\frac{\text{Cost of food consumed}}{\text{Average inventory value}} = \text{Food inventory turnover}$$

- Note that it is cost of food consumed rather than cost of food sold that is used as the numerator in this ratio. This is because all food inventories should be tracked so that you can better determine what is sold, wasted, spoiled, pilfered, or provided to employees as employee meals.

- Inventory turnover is a measure of how many times an operation's total inventory value is purchased and then sold to guests.

- High inventory turnovers should be caused by increased sales and not by increased food waste, food spoilage, or employee theft.

- The average inventory value used as the denominator in the food inventory turnover formula is computed by adding beginning inventory for this period to the ending inventory from this period and dividing by 2, as follows:

$$\frac{\text{Beginning inventory value} + \text{Ending inventory value}}{2} = \text{Average inventory value}$$

- Managers can compute an overall food inventory turnover or they can compute inventory turnovers for each of his food categories.

6. Analysis of Beverage Expense

- Beverage inventory turnover is computed using the following formula:

$$\frac{\text{Cost of beverages consumed}}{\text{Average inventory value}} = \text{Beverage inventory turnover}$$

- If an operation carries a large number of rare and expensive wines, it will find that its beverage inventory turnover rate is relatively low. Conversely, those beverage operations that sell their products primarily by the glass are likely to experience wine inventory turnover rates that are quite high.

- Similar to the method for adjusting sales, the method for adjusting expense categories for known cost increases is as follows:

  Step 1. Increase prior-period expense by amount of cost increase.
  Step 2. Determine appropriate sales data, remembering to adjust prior-period sales, if applicable.
  Step 3. Divide costs determined in Step 1 above by sales determined in Step 2 above.

- All food and beverage expense categories must be adjusted both in terms of costs and selling price if effective comparisons are to be made over time.

- As product costs increase or decrease, and as menu prices change, so too may food and beverage expense percentages change.

7. Analysis of Labor Expense

- When total dollar sales volume increases, fixed labor cost percentages will decline.

- Variable labor costs will increase along with sales volume increases, but the percentage of revenue they consume should stay constant.

- When you combine a declining percentage (fixed labor cost) with a constant one (variable labor cost), you should achieve a reduced overall labor percentage when revenue rises, but your total labor dollars expended will be higher.

- Serving additional guests will most often cost operation additional (variable cost) labor dollars.

- Declining costs of labor may be the result of significant reductions in the number of guests served. That is not desirable.

- Just as adjustments must be made for changes in food and beverage expenses before valid expense comparisons can be made, so too must adjustments be made for changes, if any, in the price an operator pays for labor such as a **COLA** (cost of living adjustment), or for raises.

- To estimate future labor costs, adjust both sales and cost of labor using the same steps as those employed for adjusting food or beverage cost percentage and you will be able to compute a new labor cost as follows:

  Step 1. Determine sales adjustment.
  Step 2. Determine total labor cost adjustment.
  Step 3. Compute adjusted labor cost percentage.

- This year's projected labor cost is then computed as follows:

This year's sales × Last year's adjusted labor cost % = This year's projected labor cost

---

- Increases in payroll taxes, benefit programs, and employee turnover will all affect labor cost percentage.

- One of the fastest-increasing labor-related costs for foodservice managers today is cost of health insurance benefit programs.

- The Patient Protection and Affordable Care Act (**Affordable Care Act**) is the federal law mandating, in some situations, that foodservice employers provide health care insurance for their employees.

8. Analysis of Other Expenses

- An analysis of other expenses should be performed each time the P&L is produced.

- For comparison purposes, managers are able to use industry trade publications to get national averages on other expense categories. One helpful source is an annual publication, the *Restaurant Industry Operations Report* published by the National Restaurant Association and prepared by the Deloitte & Touche accounting firm. It can be ordered through the National Restaurant Association's website.

- For operations that are a part of a corporate chain, unit managers can receive comparison data from district and regional managers who can chart a manager's performance against those of other operators in the city, region, state, and nation.

9. Analysis of Profits

- In addition to being evaluated on the basis of their ability to generate profit dollars, foodservice managers are often evaluated on their ability to achieve targeted profit percentages, called profit margins.

- Profit percentage (profit margin) is calculated using the profit margin formula:

$$\frac{\text{Net income}}{\text{Total sales}} = \text{Profit margin}$$

- **Profit margin** is also known as **return on sales**, or **ROS**. For the foodservice manager, perhaps no number is more important than ROS. This percentage is the most telling indicator of a manager's overall effectiveness at generating revenues and controlling costs in line with forecasted results.

- While it is not possible to state what a "good" ROS figures should be for all restaurants, industry averages, depending on the specific segment, range from 1 percent to over 20 percent.

- Some operators prefer to use operating income (see Figure 9.1) as the numerator for profit margin instead of net income. This is because interest and income taxes are considered nonoperating expenses and thus, not truly reflective of a manager's ability to generate a profit.

- Profit variance % for the year can be measured by the following formula:

$$\frac{\text{Net income this period} - \text{Net income last period}}{\text{Net income last period}} = \text{Percentage variance}$$

- Monitoring selling price, guest counts, sales per guest, operating days, special events, and actual operating costs is necessary for accurate profit comparisons. Without knowledge of each of these areas, the effective analysis of profits becomes a risky proposition.

- Perceptive foodservice operators now clearly recognize that profits, planet, and people all benefit from an operation's green commitment.

- "Planet friendly" management yields many positive financial outcomes for businesses, as well as for the health of the local communities these businesses count on to support them.

- Buying local (to minimize transportation costs and environmental impact) creates relationships with those who produce food and keeps money flowing through a local economy, resulting in a healthier community and reduced health-care costs.

10. Technology Tools

- This chapter introduced the concept of management analysis as it relates to sales, expenses, and profits. In this area, software is quite advanced and the tools available to help you with your own analyses are many. The best of the programs on the market will help you:

  1. Analyze operating trends (sales and costs) over management-established time periods.

2. Analyze food and beverage costs.
3. Analyze labor costs.
4. Analyze other expenses.
5. Analyze profits.
6. Compare operating results of multiple profit centers within one location or across several locations.
7. Interface with an operation's point-of-sale (POS) system or even incorporate it completely.
8. "Red flag" areas of potential management concern.
9. Evaluate the financial productivity of individual servers, day parts, or other specific time periods established by management.
10. Compare actual to budgeted results and compute variance percentages as well as suggest revisions to future budget periods based on current operating results.

Key Terms & Concepts Review

Match the key terms with their correct definitions.

1. Cost accounting _____ a. A professional designation indicating the passing of a standardized examination (The Uniform Certified Public Accountant Examination) demonstrating the highest levels of competency in accounting.

2. Managerial accounting _____ b. A recommended and standardized (uniform) set of accounting procedures used for categorizing and reporting revenue and expense.

3. Bookkeeping _____ c. Often referred to as profit margin. This formula refers to net income divided by total revenues. Can also be stated in whole dollar terms.

4. Certified management accountant (CMA) _____ d. The profit realized after all expenses and appropriate taxes for a business have been paid.

5. Certified public accountant (CMA) _____ e. A term utilized in the *Uniform System of Accounts for Restaurants* (*USAR*) indicating an operation's remaining revenue after subtracting all of its operating expenses but before subtracting the amounts of any income taxes that are due.

6. Sarbanes–Oxley Act (SOX) _____ f. The process of documenting and analyzing sales, expenses, and profits.

7. Uniform system of accounts _____ g. A professional designation and certification program designed for accounting and financial management professionals and administered by the Institute of Management Accountants, Inc.

8. Net income _____ h. A term utilized in the *Uniform System of Accounts for Restaurants* (*USAR*) indicating an operation's remaining revenue after subtracting all operating expenses except costs those designated as corporate overhead, interest expense, and other income (expense).

9. Prime cost _____ i. A term used to describe a raise in employee pay.

10. Restaurant operating income _____ j. List of all details associated with each line item on the income statement.

11. Income before income taxes _____ k. The number of times the total value of inventory has been purchased and replaced in an accounting period.

12. Aggregate statement _____ l. Formally known as The Patient Protection and Affordable Care Act; the federal law designed to expand health-care coverage for US citizens.

13. Supporting schedules _____ m. Technically known as the Public Company Accounting Reform and Investor Protection Act, the law provides criminal penalties for those found to have committed accounting fraud. It covers a whole range of corporate governance issues, including the regulation of those who are assigned the task of verifying a company's financial health.

14. Gross profit _____ n. This formula refers to net income divided by total revenues. Also referred to as return on sales (ROS).

15. Inventory turnover	_____	o.	Summary of all details associated with the sales, costs, and profits of a foodservice establishment.
16. Cost of living adjustment (COLA)	_____	p.	The process of recording and summarizing financial data.
17. Affordable Care Act	_____	q.	An operation's total cost of sales added to its total labor cost.
18. Profit margin	_____	r.	Covers Sales through Total Gross Profit on the *Uniform System of Accounts for Restaurants* income statement. Consists of food and beverage sales and costs that can and should be controlled by the manager on a daily basis.
19. Return on sales (ROS)	_____	s.	The process of documenting and analyzing sales, expenses, and profits. Sometimes referred to as cost accounting.

Discussion Questions

1. Identify and describe the importance of the system of accounts that the National Restaurant Association has developed.

   _____

   _____

   _____

   _____

2. Explain what the income statement is, and identify the four sections that make up this statement.

   _____

   _____

   _____

   _____

3. Identify and define the act that was passed by the US Congress in 2002 regarding fraudulently reported financial information.

   _____

   _____

   _____

   _____

4. List the six areas of the income statement that a manager should analyze.

   _____

   _____

   _____

   _____

5. List and describe the two management characteristics that are commonly evaluated by an assessment of an operation's profit margin.

   _____

   _____

   _____

   _____

Quiz Yourself

Choose the letter of the best answer to the questions listed below.

1. What is another term sometimes used to identify managerial accounting?
   a. bookkeeping
   b. tax accounting
   c. cost accounting
   d. financial accounting

2. Which term refers to the recording and summarizing of financial data?
   a. Bookkeeping
   b. Tax accounting
   c. Cost accounting
   d. Financial accounting

3. Which term refers to the analysis of a business's monthly financial operating results?
   a. bookkeeping
   b. tax accounting
   c. financial accounting
   d. managerial accounting

4. What do the initials "CPA" refer to in a business environment?
   a. certified public analyst
   b. certified personal analyst
   c. certified public accountant
   d. certified personal accountant

5. A primary purpose of the Sarbanes–Oxley Act (SOX) was to
   a. penalize accounting fraud.
   b. mandate consistency in financial reporting.
   c. ensure timely reporting of financial results.
   d. train managers in proper accounting procedures.

6. The purpose of a uniform system of accounts is to encourage consistency in the reporting of financial information.
   a. True
   b. False

7. There is one uniform system of accounts for use by all segments of the hospitality industry.
   a. True
   b. False

8. The National Restaurant Association (NRA) was involved in the development of the USAR.
   a. True
   b. False

9. Restaurants must report their operating data in the USAR format.
   a. True
   b. False

10. For best results, small restaurants should use the USAR in the same way it is used in large restaurants.
    a. True
    b. False

11. What is another name for an operation's P&L statement?
    a. balance sheet
    b. income summary
    c. income statement
    d. statement of cash flows

12. A manager is preparing her P&L using the USAR. Which item will she list first on the P&L?
    a. profits
    b. revenue
    c. food cost
    d. labor cost

13. Net income is the profit generated by a business after all its appropriate expenses have been
    a. paid.
    b. incurred.
    c. recorded.
    d. analyzed.

14. How many major sections are contained in a P&L prepared according to *USAR* recommendations?
    a. 2
    b. 3
    c. 4
    d. 5

15. The main sections in a P&L prepared according to *USAR* recommendations are listed from
    a. least variable to most variable.
    b. most variable to least variable.
    c. least controllable to most controllable.
    d. most controllable to least controllable.

16. An operation's prime costs include its total cost of sales and its total
    a. labor costs.
    b. occupancy costs.
    c. non-controllable expenses
    d. other controllable expenses.

17. On a P&L prepared using the *USAR* format, which ratios are NOT calculated as a percentage of total sales?
    a. labor costs
    b. occupancy costs
    c. food and beverage costs
    d. non-controllable expenses

18. Where do managers list detailed information regarding expenses incurred in the operation of their businesses?
    a. balance sheet
    b. income statement
    c. supporting schedules
    d. statement of cash flows

19. Foodservice operators can measure their sales in terms of either dollars or
    a. net income.
    b. gross revenue.
    c. check averages.
    d. number of customers served.

20. Last year, a quick service manager's sales were $780,000. This year, the manager's sales were $873,600. What was the manager's sales variance percentage this year compared to last year?
    a. 11%
    b. 12%
    c. 13%
    d. 14%

21. Last year, a food cart owner's sales were $480,000. This year, the cart owner's sales were $450,000. What was the owner's sales variance percentage this year compared to last year?
    a. −62.5%
    b. −6.25%
    c. 6.25%
    d. 62.5%

22. Last year, a steakhouse manager's sales were $1,525,000. This year, the manager increased menu prices by 5 percent and achieved sales of $1,745,500. What was the manager's actual sales percentage increase after adjusting for the menu price increase?
    a. 3%
    b. 5%
    c. 7%
    d. 9%

23. When comparing revenue in one accounting period to that in another period, managers must make sure that
    a. the menu items sold were identical.
    b. the number of guests served is identical.
    c. differences in the time periods' characteristics are ignored.
    d. differences in the time periods' characteristics are considered.

24. What is the denominator in the food cost percentage formula?
    a. Total sales
    b. Food sales
    c. Variable sales
    d. Food and beverage sales

25. One week, a sandwich shop manager had sales of $6,000, bread cost of $480, vegetable cost of $250, meat cost of $750, and all other food costs of $100. What was the manager's bread cost percentage for the week?
    a. 0.8%
    b. 2.6%
    c. 8.0%
    d. 26.3%

26. What is the formula that managers use to calculate their gross profit?
    a. Total Sales + Total Cost of Sales = Gross Profit
    b. Total Sales – Total Cost of Sales = Gross Profit
    c. Total Sales × Total Cost of Sales = Gross Profit
    d. Total Sales ÷ Total Cost of Sales = Gross Profit

27. Which formula calculates an operation's average inventory value?
    a. Beginning inventory ÷ 2
    b. (Beginning inventory – ending inventory) ÷ 2
    c. (Beginning inventory × ending inventory) ÷ 2
    d. (Beginning inventory + ending inventory) ÷ 2

28. What is the numerator in the food inventory turnover formula?
    a. Revenue
    b. Cost of food sold
    c. Cost of food consumed
    d. Average inventory value

29. Last year a sports bar had beginning beverage inventory of $12,000, ending beverage inventory of $16,000, beverage sales of $800,000 and it achieved a 20 percent cost of beverage consumed. How many times did this operation turn its beverage inventory last year?
    a. 9.4 times
    b. 11.4 times
    c. 14.9 times
    d. 18.4 times

30. Which beverage product category should have the highest number of inventory turns?
    a. beer
    b. spirits
    c. liqueurs
    d. rare wines

31. Which beverage product category should have the least number of inventory turns?
    a. beer
    b. spirits
    c. liqueurs
    d. rare wines

32. What should be the impact on beverage costs (BC) and beverage cost percentage (BC%) if an operation attracts more guests and, as a result, sells more beverage products?
    a. BC increases, BC% increases
    b. BC increases, BC% decreases
    c. BC increases, BC% stays the same
    d. BC stays the same, BC% stays the same

33. To properly compare food and beverage expense category percentages over long periods of time, appropriate adjustments must be made in terms of product costs and
    a. selling prices
    b. gross profit margins
    c. number of units sold
    d. item contribution margins

34. A manager's operation has both fixed and variable labor costs. What will be the impact on fixed cost (FC) and fixed cost percentage (FC%) spent for labor if the manager increases the operation's sales by serving more guests?
    a. FC increases and FC% increases
    b. FC increases and FC% decreases
    c. FC is unchanged and FC% decreases
    d. FC is unchanged and FC% is unchanged

35. A manager's operation has both fixed and variable labor costs. What will be the impact on labor variable cost (VC) and variable cost percentage (VC%) if the manager increases the operation's sales by serving more guests?
    a. VC increases and VC% increases
    b. VC decreases and VC% decreases
    c. VC increases and VC% is unchanged
    d. VC decreases and VC% is unchanged

36. A manager's operation has both fixed and variable labor costs. What will be the impact on labor's fixed cost percentage (FC%) and variable cost percentage (VC%) if the manager increases the operation's sales by serving more guests?
    a. FC% increases and VC% increases
    b. FC% decreases and VC% decreases
    c. FC% increases and VC% is unchanged
    d. FC% decreases and VC% is unchanged

37. A manager's sales increased 10 percent this year compared to last year. At the beginning of this year, the manager gave all employees a 5 percent raise. What should have happened to the manager's fixed labor cost percentage (FC%) and variable labor cost percentage (VC%) this year compared to last year?
    a. FC% increases and VC% increases
    b. FC% decreases and VC% decreases
    c. FC% increases and VC% is unchanged
    d. FC% decreases and VC% is unchanged

38. Last year, a manager achieved sales of $1,000,000 and a total labor cost of 30 percent. This year, the manager raised prices by 5 percent and gave employee raises and benefit increases that together will equal 2 percent of last year's labor cost. If there are no changes in labor efficiency, what should be this manager's (rounded) labor cost percentage for next year?
    a. 28%
    b. 29%
    c. 30%
    d. 31%

39. In the past decade, which labor expense category had the fastest-rising costs for foodservice operators?
    a. wages
    b. FICA taxes
    c. health insurance
    d. 401(k) contributions

40. An analysis of other expenses should be performed each time an operation's income statement is produced.
    a. True
    b. False

41. When using the USAR format, an operation's occupancy costs are classified as a non-controllable other expense.
    a. True
    b. False

42. When using the USAR format, an operation's utility costs are classified as a non-controllable other expense.
    a. True
    b. False

43. Leasing a piece of equipment for use in its kitchen would increase an operation's other controllable expenses.
    a. True
    b. False

44. Managers operating chain restaurant units can get comparison data on other expense costs in similar units from their district and regional chain managers.
    a. True
    b. False

45. The profit margin achieved in an operation is equal to the operation's
    a. Net income ÷ Total sales.
    b. Total sales ÷ Net income.
    c. Gross profit ÷ Total sales.
    d. Prime costs ÷ Net income.

46. An operation's profit margin is identical to its
    a. net income.
    b. prime costs.
    c. return on sales.
    d. total contribution margin.

47. What is the typical ROS percentage for a profitable foodservice operation?
    a. less than 2%
    b. 2% to 20%
    c. 21% to 50%
    d. more than 50%

48. A manager's operation generated net income last year of $161,500. This year the manager's net income was $169,575. What was the percentage increase in net income achieved by the manager this year?
    a. 0.05%
    b. 2.5%
    c. 5.0%
    d. 25%

49. A manager's operation generated net income last year of $350,500. This year, the operation experienced a 4 percent increase in net income. What was the operation's net income this year?
    a. $344,520
    b. $364,520
    c. $384,520
    d. $404,520

Chapter Answers to Key Terms & Concepts Review, Discussion Questions, and Quiz Yourself

Key Terms & Concepts Review

1. f	6. m	11. e	16. i
2. s	7. b	12. o	17. l
3. p	8. d	13. j	18. n
4. g	9. q	14. r	19. c
5. a	10. h	15. k	

Discussion Questions

1. Identify and describe the importance of the system of accounts that the National Restaurant Association has developed.

   - Financial reports related to the operation of a foodservice facility are of great interest to management, stockholders, owners, creditors, governmental agencies, and, often, the general public.
   - To ensure that the financial information reported for businesses can be easily understood, and is presented in a way that is both useful and consistent, uniform systems of accounts have been established for many areas of the hospitality industry.
   - The *Uniform System of Accounts for Restaurants* (*USAR*) has been developed in conjunction with the National Restaurant Association (NRA) for the purpose of identifying a standardized set of procedures useful for categorizing revenue and expenses in the restaurant industry.

2. Explain what the income statement is, and identify the four sections that make up this statement.
   - Income statement: A detailed listing of revenue and expenses for a defined time period (accounting period.)
   - The income statement is formally known as the "Statement of Income and Expense" but is informally referred to as the Profit and Loss Statement, and even less formally as the P&L.
   - The four major portions of the P&L are:
     - Sales section: This is the revenue generated by a business in a specific accounting period.
     - Prime costs section: This consists of food and beverage expenses and labor costs that can and should be controlled by a manager.
     - Other Controllable Expenses section: These are those costs under the control of the manager but on more of a weekly or monthly basis.
     - Non-Controllable Expenses section: These expenses are least controllable by the foodservice manager. This section also details "income before income taxes," "income taxes," and "net income," which is also referred to as net profit after taxes.

3. Identify and define the act that was passed by the US Congress in 2002 regarding fraudulently reported financial information.
   - It is essential that a business's operating results be presented in an honest and transparent manner.
   - The Sarbanes–Oxley Act (SOX), technically known as the Public Company Accounting Reform and Investor Protection Act, is a law that provides criminal penalties for those found to have committed accounting fraud.

4. List the six areas of the income statement that a manager should analyze.
   - Sales/volume
   - Food expense
   - Beverage expense
   - Labor expense
   - Other controllable and non-controllable expense
   - Profits

5. List and describe the two management characteristics that are commonly evaluated by an assessment of an operation's profit margin.
   - Those who assess managers' skill know that the profit formula:

$$Revenue - Expense = Profits$$

   is one of the most important formulas in the world of business. This is so because most businesses are operated the purpose of making a profit.

   - The two major factors affecting profitability of a business are revenue and expense.

     1. The format of a properly prepared income statement lists revenue first. This is done to indicate the importance of sales to a business's profitability. When sales are too low in a business, is very difficult to generate a reasonable profit margin. Therefore, a major characteristic assessed by an evaluation of an operation's profit margin is a manager's ability to generate sales.

     2. While the generation of sufficient revenue is an important factor when determining an operation's profit margin, control of the operation's expenses is equally important. High levels of volume with poor expense control will most often yield insufficient profit margins.

     Alternatively, when total revenue levels are restricted, but expenses are well-controlled, sufficient profit margins may still be achievable. Therefore, a second major characteristic assessed by an evaluation of an operation's profit margin is the manager's ability to control expenses.

Quiz Yourself

1. c.	14. c.	27. d.	40. a.
2. a.	15. d.	28. c.	41. a.
3. d.	16. a.	29. b.	42. b.
4. c.	17. c.	30. a.	43. b.
5. a.	18. c.	31. d.	44. a.
6. a.	19. d.	32. c.	45. a.
7. b.	20. b.	33. a.	46. c.
8. a.	21. b.	34. c.	47. b.
9. b.	22. d.	35. c.	48. c.
10. b.	23. d.	36. c.	49. b.
11. c.	24. b.	37. b.	
12. a.	25. c.	38. b.	
13. a.	26. b.	39. c.	

Chapter 10

Planning for Profit

Learning Outcomes

At the conclusion of this chapter, you will be able to:

- Analyze a menu for profitability.

    In most cases, when customers think about a foodservice operation, they think about the operation's menu and the specific types of menu items it sells. As a result, the menu is a powerful marketing tool for attracting customers. But a menu must do more. The menu must be designed and priced in such a way as to optimize the financial performance of a foodservice business. To assess a menu's ability to do that, managers must be adept at analyzing their menus for profitability.

    While there is more than one method that can be used to analyze a menu for profitability, all managers must be able to choose and apply one or more of these methods to assist them in performing this important task.

- Prepare a Cost/Volume/Profit (break-even) analysis.

    Revenue – Expense = Profits is a fundamental business equation. Because all businesses incur fixed costs, it follows that a minimum amount of sales must be generated if the businesses is to secure enough income to pay for all of its fixed and variable operating costs. Only after fixed and variable costs of operating have been fully paid will a business generate a profit.

    A Cost/Volume/Profit (break-even) analysis is the tool managers use to identify their break-even point: the point at which revenue equals the sum of fixed and variable costs. All managers should learn how to utilize this important tool.

- Establish a budget and monitor performance to the budget.

    It is been said that the best managers can foretell the future. While that may not be entirely true, it certainly is true that the best managers seek to accurately predict future revenue, expenses and profits in their businesses. When managers do that in a formal way, they create a budget. The ability to establish a budget and to monitor an operation's performance relative to that budget is necessary so that managers can identify specific areas in which budget modifications should be made or operational improvements should be undertaken.

Study Notes

1. Financial Analysis and Profit Planning

- In addition to analyzing their P&L statements (see Chapter 10), managers should also undertake a thorough examination of three additional operational areas that will assist them in planning for profit.

- These three areas of analysis are:

    - Menu analysis
    - Cost/Volume/Profit (CVP) analysis
    - Budgeting

- Menu analysis concerns itself with the profitability of the menu items you will sell.

- CVP analysis addresses the sales (revenue) dollars required by your foodservice unit to avoid an operating loss and to make a profit.

- Budgeting allows managers to plan their next year or next period's operating results by projecting sales, expenses, and profits and then using that information to develop a budgeted (forecasted) P&L statement.

- The best managers know that pre-planning by addressing these areas is the key to achieving the cost and profit goals that will keep their operations in business.

2. Menu Analysis

- Effective managers want to know the answer to a basic operational question: "How does the sale of a particular menu item contribute to the overall success of my operation?" The answer to such a question can sometimes be provided by applying mathematics, but numbers are only one component of menu analysis. There are other factors to consider.

- Menu analysis also involves marketing, sociology, psychology, and emotions. Remember that guests respond best not to weighty financial analyses, but rather to menu item descriptions, the placement of items on the menu, their price, and their current popularity.

- Many components of the menu such as pricing, layout, design, and menu copy (item descriptions) play an important role in the overall success of a foodservice operation.

- When assessing the most popular menu analysis systems in wide use, you will find that all of these systems seek to perform a menu analysis using one or more of the following operational variables:

  - Food cost percentage
  - Item popularity
  - Contribution margin
  - Selling price
  - Variable expenses
  - Fixed expenses

- Three of the most popular systems of menu analysis are:
  1. Food cost %
  2. Contribution margin
  3. Goal value analysis

- The method (name), variables considered, analysis methodology and assessment goals of these three systems are summarized below:

Three Methods of Menu Analysis Summary

Method	Variables Considered	Analysis Method	Goal
1. Food cost %	a. Food cost % b. Popularity	Matrix	Minimize overall food cost %
2. Contribution margin	a. Contribution margin b. Popularity	Matrix	Maximize contribution margin
3. Goal value analysis	a. Contribution margin % b. Popularity c. Selling price d. Variable cost % e. Food cost %	Algebraic equation	Achieve predetermined profit % goals

- **Matrix analysis** (see above summary) refers to a system of menu analysis designed to provide a comparison between menu items.

- A matrix allows menu items to be placed into categories based on whether they are above or below menu item averages for specific factors such as food cost percentage, popularity, and contribution margin.

- Menu analysis that focuses on food cost percentage is the oldest and most traditional method of menu analysis used.

- When analyzing a menu using the food cost percentage method, you are seeking to identify those menu items that will have the effect of minimizing your operation's overall food cost percentage.

- The food cost percentage method of menu analysis uses a 2×2 matrix as an assessment tool. In this system menu items are categorized based on two variables:

    - Food cost percentage
    - Popularity (number sold)

Food Cost % Menu Analysis Matrix

		Popularity	
		Low	High
Food Cost %	High	1 High food cost % Low popularity	2 High food cost % High popularity
	Low	3 Low food cost % Low popularity	4 Low food cost % High popularity

- Based on known information about an item's food cost percentage and sales levels (popularity), each menu item is assigned to one square in the matrix. The specific characteristics of the menu items that fall into each of the four matrix squares are unique.

- When developing a menu that seeks to minimize food cost percentage, items in the fourth square are the most desirable because the low food cost percentage of these items helps keep the operation's overall food cost percentage low. Items in square four also sell very well.

- In spite of its popularity, the food cost percentage menu analysis method has limitations in that it does not directly consider the profit resulting from the sale of individual menu items.

- When analyzing a menu using the contribution margin approach, the operator seeks to produce a menu that maximizes the menu's overall contribution margin.

- **Contribution margin (per menu item)** is defined as the amount that remains after the product cost of a menu item is subtracted from the menu item's selling price.

- Contribution margin per menu item is calculated as:

Selling price – Product cost = Contribution margin per menu item

- To determine the total contribution margin for the menu, the following formula is used:

Total sales – Total product costs =Total contribution margin

- You can determine the average contribution margin per item, using the following formula:

$$\frac{\text{Total contribution margin}}{\text{Number of items sold}} = \text{Average contribution margin per item}$$

- Contribution margin is the amount that you will have available to pay for your labor and other expenses and to keep for a profit.

- When contribution margin is the driving factor in analyzing a menu, the two variables used for the analysis are:

1. Contribution margin
2. Item popularity

Contribution Margin Menu Analysis Matrix

Popularity

		Low	High
Contribution Margin	High	1 High contribution margin Low popularity	2 High contribution margin High popularity
	Low	3 Low contribution margin Low popularity	4 Low contribution margin High popularity

- Each of the menu items that fall into a specific square requires a special marketing strategy.

Contribution Margin Analysis Marketing Strategy

Square	Characteristics	Problem	Marketing Strategy
1	High contribution margin Low popularity	Marginal due to lack of sales	a. Relocate on menu for greater visibility. b. Consider reducing selling price.
2	High contribution margin High popularity	None	a. Promote well. b. Increase prominence on the menu.
3	Low contribution margin Low popularity	Marginal due to both low contribution margin and lack of sales	a. Remove from menu. b. Consider offering as a special occasionally, but at a higher menu price.
4	Low contribution margin High popularity	Marginal due to low contribution margin	a. Increase price. b. Reduce prominence on the menu. c. Consider reducing portion size.

- Some users of the contribution margin method of menu analysis refer to it as **menu engineering** and they identify the squares used in the analysis by using colorful names. The most common of these are:

  - Plow horses (square 1), because these items have high contribution margins but are less popular

  - "Stars" (square 2), because these items are popular and also have high contribution margins

  - Dogs (square 3), because these have low contribution margins and are not popular

  - "Puzzles" (or sometimes "challenges") (square 4), because these menu items are highly popular but return lower than average contribution margins to the operator.

- A frequent and legitimate criticism of the contribution margin approach to menu analysis is that it tends to favor high-priced menu items over low-priced ones, because higher priced menu items, in general, tend to have the highest contribution margins.

- The selection of either food cost percentage or contribution margin as a menu analysis technique is really an attempt by the foodservice operator to answer the following questions:

    1. Are my menu items priced correctly?
    2. Are the individual menu items selling well enough to warrant keeping them on the menu?
    3. Is the overall profit margin on my menu items satisfactory?

- Because of the limitations of matrix analysis, neither the matrix food cost nor the matrix contribution margin approach alone is truly effective in analyzing menus. This is so because, mathematically, the axes on the matrix are determined by the mean (average) of food cost percentage, contribution margin or sales level (popularity).

- When using matrix analysis, some items will always fall into the less desirable categories. This is so because, in matrix analysis, high food cost percentage, for instance, really means food cost percentage <u>above</u> that operation's average, or arithmetic mean. Obviously, then, some items must always fall above and <u>below</u> the average regardless of their contribution to operational profitability. Eliminating the poorest items only shifts other items into undesirable categories.

- Goal value analysis uses the power of an algebraic formula to replace less sophisticated menu averaging techniques.

- The advantages of goal value analysis are many, including ease of use, accuracy, and the ability to simultaneously consider more variables than is possible with two-dimensional matrix analysis.

- **Goal value analysis** does evaluate each menu item's food cost percentage, contribution margin, and popularity, but unlike the two previous analysis methods introduced it includes an analysis of the menu item's nonfood variable costs as well as the item's selling price.

- Menu items that achieve goal values higher than that of the menu's overall goal value will contribute greater than average profit percentages. As the goal value for an item increases, so too, does its profitability percentage.

- The goal value formula is:

$A \times B \times C \times D$ = Goal value
where
A = 1.00 – Food cost %
B = Item popularity
C = Selling price
D = 1.00 – (Variable cost % + Food cost %)

- The computed goal value carries no unit designation; that is, it is neither a percentage nor a dollar figure because it is really a numerical target or score.

- Every menu will have items that are more or less profitable than others.

- A **loss leader** is a menu item that is priced very low, sometimes even below total costs, for the purpose of drawing large numbers of guests to the operation.

- Items that do not achieve the targeted goal value tend to be deficient in one or more of the key areas of food cost percentage, popularity, selling price, or variable cost percentage.

- In theory and in practice, all menu items have the potential of reaching the goal value.

- Managers can use the goal value formula to solve for unknowns:

Solving for Goal Value Unknowns

Known Variables	Unknown Variables	Method to Find Unknown
A, B, C, D	Goal value (GV)	$A \times B \times C \times D$
B, C, D, GV	A	$GV / B \times C \times D$
A, C, D, GV	B	$GV / A \times C \times D$
A, B, D, GV	C	$GV / A \times B \times D$
A, B, C, GV	D	$GV / A \times B \times C$

- Goal value analysis will allow you to make better decisions more quickly. Goal value analysis is also powerful because it is not, as is matrix analysis, dependent on past performance to establish profitability but can be used by management to establish future menu item targets.

- A purely quantitative approach to menu analysis is neither practical nor desirable. Menu analysis and pricing decisions are always a matter of experience, skill, insight and educated predicting.

3. Cost/Volume/Profit Analysis
- Each foodservice operator knows that some accounting periods are more profitable than others. Often, this is because sales volume is higher or costs are lower during certain periods. Profitability, then, can be viewed as existing on a graph similar to the following:

Cost/Volume/Profit Graph

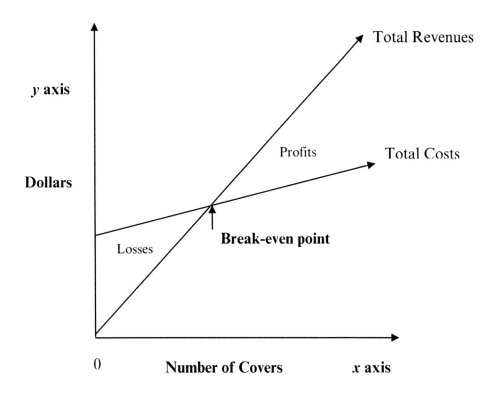

- At the **break-even point**, operational expenses are exactly equal to sales revenue; below the break-even point, costs are higher than revenues, so losses occur; above the break-even point, revenues exceed costs, so profits are made.

- A **cost/volume/profit (CVP) analysis** helps predict the sales dollars and volume required to achieve desired *profit* (or break-even) based on your known costs.

- CVP calculations can be done on either:

  1. The dollar sales volume required to break even or achieve the desired profit, or
  2. The number of guests (covers) required that must be served to break even.

- A **contribution margin income statement** simply shows P&L items in terms of sales, variable costs, contribution margin, fixed costs, before-tax profit, taxes, and and after-tax profit.

- **Contribution margin for the overall operation** is defined as the dollar amount that is *contributed* to covering fixed costs and providing for a profit.

- Recall that contribution margin is calculated as follows:

$$\text{Total sales} - \text{Variable costs} = \text{Contribution margin}$$

- To determine the dollar sales required to break even, use the following formula:

$$\frac{\text{Fixed costs}}{\text{Contribution margin \%}} = \text{Break-even point in sales}$$

- In terms of the number of guests that must be served in order to break even, use the following formula:

$$\frac{\text{Fixed costs}}{\text{Contribution margin per unit (per guest)}} = \text{Break-even point in guests served}$$

- To determine sales dollars and covers to achieve the after-tax profit goal, use the following formula:

$$\frac{\text{Fixed costs} + \text{Before-tax profit}}{\text{Contribution margin \%}} = \text{Sales dollars to achieve desired after-tax profit}$$

- To convert after-tax profit to before-tax profit, compute the following:

$$\frac{\text{After-tax profit}}{1 - \text{Tax rate}} = \text{Before-tax profit}$$

- In terms of calculating the number of guests that must be served in order to make the desired after-tax profit, use the following formula:

$$\frac{\text{Fixed costs} + \text{Before-tax profit}}{\text{Contribution margin per unit (guest)}} = \text{Guests to be served to achieve desired after-tax profit}$$

- When calculating sales and covers to achieve break-even and desired after-tax profits, you can easily remember which formulas to use if you know the following:

  1. Contribution margin *percentage* is used to calculate sales *dollars*.
  2. Contribution margin per *unit* is used to calculate sales volume in *units* (guests).
- Once you fully understand the CVP analysis concepts, you can predict any sales level for break-even or after-tax profits based on your selling price, fixed costs, variable costs, and contribution margin.

- Cost/volume/profit analysis is used to establish targets for the entire operation, whereas goal value analysis evaluates individual menu items against those operational targets. Therefore, the two analyses can be strategically linked.

Cost/Volume/Profit Analysis	Goal Value Analysis
Food cost % from contribution margin income statement	Food cost % goal
Guests served to achieve desired after-tax profit	Total average number of covers per menu item goal
Selling price	Selling price goal
Labor and other variable cost % from contribution margin income statement	Variable cost % goal

- By looking at these two analyses, you can learn how the overall goals of the operation affect menu item profitability. Conversely, you can see how changes you make to menu items affect the overall profitability of the operation.

- **Minimum sales point (MSP)** is the sales volume required to justify staying open for a given period of time.

- The information needed to calculate a MSP is:
  1. Food cost percentage
  2. Minimum payroll cost needed for the time period
  3. Variable cost percentage

- Fixed costs are eliminated from the calculation because even if volume of sales equals zero, fixed costs still exist and must be paid.

- In calculating MSP, Food cost % + Variable cost % is called the **minimum operating cost**.

- The MSP formula options are:

$$\frac{\text{Minimum labor cost}}{1-\text{Minimum operating cost}}=\text{MSP}$$

or

$$\frac{\text{Minimum labor cost}}{1 - (\text{Food cost \% + Variable cost \%})} = \text{MSP}$$

- Corporate policy, contractual hours, promotion of a new unit, competition, and other factors must all be taken into account before the decision is made to modify operational hours.

4. The Budget

- The **budget**, or financial plan, will detail the operational direction of your unit and your expected (forecasted) financial results.

- The budget should not be a static document. It should be modified and fine-tuned as managerial accounting methods present data about sales and costs that affect the direction of the overall operation.

- Just as the P&L tells you about your past performance, the budget is developed to help you achieve your future goals.

> Budgeted revenue – Budgeted expenses = Budgeted profit

- To prepare the budget and stay within it assures you achieve predetermined results.

- There are many reasons to prepare a formal budget:

  - It is the best means of analyzing alternative courses of action and allows management to examine alternatives prior to adopting a particular one.
  - It forces management to examine the facts regarding what must be done to achieve desired profit levels.
  - It provides a standard for comparison, which is essential for good controls.
  - It allows management to anticipate and prepare for future business conditions.
  - It helps management to periodically carry out a self-evaluation of the organization and its progress toward its financial objectives.
  - It provides a communication channel whereby the organization's objectives are passed along to its various departments.
  - It encourages department managers who have participated in the preparation of the budget to establish their own operating objectives and evaluation techniques and tools.
  - It provides management with reasonable estimates of future expense levels and serves as an instrument for setting proper menu prices.
  - It identifies time periods in which operational cash flows may need to be supplemented from other sources.

- It communicates realistic financial performance to owners, investors, and the operation's managers.

- The effective foodservice operator builds a budget, monitors it closely, modifies it when necessary, and achieves desired results.

- Budgeting is best done by the entire management team, for it is only through participation in the process that the whole organization will feel compelled to support the budget.

- Foodservice budgets can be considered as one of three main types: long-range budget, annual budget, and achievement budget.

- The **long-range budget** is typically prepared for a period of three to five years.

- The **annual budget** is for a one-year period or, in some cases, one season. An annual budget need not follow a calendar year.

- An annual budget need not consist of 12, one-month periods. While many operators prefer one-month budgets, some prefer budgets consisting of thirteen, 28-day periods, while others use quarterly (three-month), monthly, or even weekly budgets to plan for revenues and costs throughout the budget year.

- The **achievement budget** is always of a shorter range, perhaps a month or a week. It provides current operating information and thus assists in making current operational decisions.

5. Developing the Budget

- To establish any type of budget, you need to have the following information available:

    1. Prior-period operating results (if available)
    2. Assumptions of next-period operations
    3. Goals
    4. Monitoring policies

- To determine a food budget, compute the estimated food cost as follows:

> 1. Last year's food cost per meal = Last year's cost of food ÷ Total meals served
>
> 2. Last year's food cost per meal + % Estimated increase in food cost = This year's food cost per meal

211

> 3. This year's food cost per meal × Number of meals to be served this year = Estimated cost of food this year

- To determine a labor budget, compute the estimated labor cost as follows:

> 1. Last year's labor cost per meal = Last year's cost of labor ÷ Total meals served
>
> 2. Last year's labor cost per meal + % Estimated increase in labor cost = This year's labor cost per meal
>
> 3. This year's labor cost per meal × Number of meals to be served this year = Estimated cost of labor this year

- Budgeting for utility costs is one of a foodservice operator's biggest challenges. This is due to both the instability of energy prices and, in many locations, the impact of weather on utilities usage.

- Strategies for reducing energy usage include:

    1. Investigating the instillation of smart lighting systems that automatically turn off lights when storage areas are vacant.
    2. Replacing all incandescent lighting with an appropriate type of electric discharge lamp (such as fluorescent, mercury vapor, metal halide, or sodium) wherever possible.
    3. Using dual-flush, low-flow or waterless toilets to reduce water waste.
    4. Installing low-flow faucet aerators on all sinks to cut water usage by as much as 40%—from a standard 4 gallons per minute to a cost-saving 2.5 gallons a minute.
    5. Implementing an effective preventive maintenance program for all cooking equipment including frequent and accurate temperature recalibrations.
    6. Reducing waste disposal costs by implementing effective source reduction plans as well as pre- and post-production recycling efforts.

6. Monitoring the Budget

- In general, the budget should be monitored in each of the following three areas:

    1. Revenue
    2. Expense
    3. Profit

- Some foodservice operators relate revenue to the number of seats they have available in their operation. The formula for the computation of sales per seat is as follows:

$$\frac{\text{Total sales}}{\text{Available seats}} = \text{Sales per seat}$$

- Some commercial foodservice operators relate revenue to the number of square feet their operations occupy. These operators budget revenues based on a **sales per square foot** basis. The formula of sales per square foot is as follows:

$$\frac{\text{Total sales}}{\text{Total square footage occupied}} = \text{Sales per square foot}$$

- Effective managers compare their actual revenue to that which they have projected on a regular basis.

- If revenue should fall below projected levels, the impact on profit can be substantial.

- Effective foodservice managers are careful to monitor operational expense because costs that are too high or too low may be cause for concern.

- Some operators elect to utilize the **yardstick method** of calculating expense standards so determinations can be made as to whether variations in expenses are due to changes in sales volume, or other reasons such as waste or theft.

- Developing Yardstick Standards for Food Costs

    Step 1. Divide total inventory into management-designated subgroups (categories); for example, meats, produce, dairy, and groceries.
    Step 2. Establish dollar value of subgroup purchases for prior accounting period.
    Step 3. Establish sales volume for the prior accounting period.
    Step 4. Determine percentage of purchasing dollar spent for each food category.
    Step 5. Determine percentage of revenue dollar spent for each food category.
    Step 6. Develop weekly sales volume and associated expense projection. Compute percentage cost to sales for each food grouping and sales estimate.
    Step 7. Compare weekly revenue and expense to projection. Correct if necessary.

- Developing Yardstick Standards for Labor Costs

  Step 1.   Divide total labor cost into management-designated subgroups, for example, cooks, ware washers, and bartenders.
  Step 2.   Establish dollar value spent for each subgroup during the prior accounting period.
  Step 3.   Establish sales volume for the prior accounting period.
  Step 4.   Determine percentage of labor dollar spent for each subgroup.
  Step 5.   Determine percentage of revenue dollar spent for each labor category.
  Step 6.   Develop weekly sales volume and associated expense projection. Compute % cost to sales for each labor category and sales estimate.
  Step 7.   Compare weekly revenue and expense to projection. Correct if necessary.

- As business conditions change, changes in the budget are to be expected. This is because budgets are based on a specific set of assumptions, and if these assumptions change, so too should the budgets be changed.

- Budgeted profit levels must be realized if an operation is to provide adequate returns for owner and investor risk.

- The primary purpose of management is to generate the profits needed to continue the business. Budgeting for these profits is a fundamental step in that process.

7. Technology Tools

- While menu analysis software is often packaged as part of a larger program and is somewhat limited, the software required to do an overall break-even analysis is readily available, as well as that required for budgeting. Specialized software in this area is available to help you:

  1. Evaluate item profitability based on:
     - Food cost %
     - Popularity
     - Contribution margin
     - Selling price
  2. Conduct menu matrix analysis.
  3. Perform break-even analysis.
  4. Budget revenue and expense levels.
  5. Budget profit levels.
  6. Assemble budgets based on days, weeks, months, years, or other identifiable accounting periods.
  7. Conduct performance to budget analysis.
  8. Maintain performance to budget histories.
  9. Blend budgets from multiple profit centers (or multiple units).
  10. Perform budgeted cash flow analysis.

- For commercial operators, it is not wise to operate a foodservice unit without a properly priced menu and an accurate budget that reflects estimated sales and expense levels.

- Accurate budgeting is just as important for noncommercial foodservice operators.

Key Terms & Concepts Review
Match the key terms with their correct definitions.

1. Matrix analysis	_____	a.	A menu pricing and analysis system that compares goals of the foodservice operation to performance of individual menu items.
2. Quick service restaurant (QSR)	_____	b.	The dollar amount that contributes to covering fixed costs and providing for a profit.
3. Menu engineering	_____	c.	The point at which operational expenses are exactly equal to sales revenue.
4. Goal value analysis	_____	d.	The total revenue generated by a facility divided by the number of seats in the dining area.
5. Loss leaders	_____	e.	A financial summary that shows P&L items in terms of sales, variable costs, contribution margin, fixed costs, and profit.
6. Break-even point	_____	f.	A specific currency denomination, for example, US dollar, British pound, or Japanese yen.
7. Cost/volume/profit (CVP) analysis	_____	g.	A method for comparisons between menu items. A matrix allows menu items to be placed into categories based on whether they are above or below overall menu item averages such as food cost %, popularity, and contribution margin.
8. Contribution margin income statement	_____	h.	Food cost % plus Variable cost %, used in calculating minimum sales point.

9. Contribution margin for overall operation _____

10. Minimum sales point (MSP) _____

11. Minimum operating cost _____

12. Long-range budget _____

13. Annual budget _____

14. Achievement budget _____

15. Monetary unit _____

16. Sales per seat _____

17. Sales per square foot _____

18. Yardstick method _____

i. A forecast or estimate of projected revenue, expense, and profit for a period of a month or a week. It provides current operating information and, thus, assists in making current operational decisions.

j. A forecast or estimate of projected revenue, expense, and profit for a period of three to five years.

k. A restaurant that offers a limited menu and is designed for the convenience of customers who want their food fast.

l. The dollar sales volume required to justify staying open.

m. Method of calculating expense standards so determinations can be made as to whether variations in expenses are due to changes in sales volume or other reasons, such as waste or theft.

n. A measure of an operation's revenue as it relates to the size of the operation. Calculated as: Total sales ÷ Total square footage.

o. A popular name for one variation of the contribution margin method of menu analysis and that classifies menu items as stars, puzzles, plow horses, or dogs.

p. A forecast or estimate of projected revenue, expense, and profit for a period of one year.

q. Menu items that are priced very low for the purpose of drawing large numbers of customers to an operation.

r. Method that helps predict the sales dollars and volume required to achieve desired profit (or break-even) based on known costs.

Discussion Questions

1. List and explain the three areas of analysis that can assist a manager in planning for profit.

   _____

   _____

   _____

   _____

2. List and briefly describe the six different operational variables that can be utilized when conducting a menu analysis.

   _____

   _____

   _____

   _____

3. Explain the importance to foodservice managers of the "minimum sales point" concept.

   _____

   _____

   _____

   _____

4. Identify and describe the three main types of foodservice budgets.

   _____

   _____

   _____

   _____

5. Explain the importance of monitoring each of the three main areas addressed in an operating budget.

   _____

   _____

   _____

   _____

Quiz Yourself

Choose the letter of the best answer to the questions listed below.

1. The three operational areas addressed in the text, and that managers must analyze in addition to their P&Ls, are menu analysis, CVP analysis, and
    a. prices.
    b. budgets.
    c. marketing.
    d. cash flows.

2. When properly performed, menu analysis seeks to identify menu item
    a. costs.
    b. popularity.
    c. profitability.
    d. selling prices.

3. Identifying the amount of sales required to avoid an operating loss is the primary purpose of
    a. CVP analysis.
    b. menu analysis.
    c. matrix analysis.
    d. goal value analysis.

4. Budgeting allows managers to predict a future account period's sales, expenses, and
    a. profits.
    b. selling prices.
    c. contribution margins.
    d. labor productivity ratios.

5. The financial document most similar to an operation's budget is its forecasted
    a. balance sheet.
    b. income statement.
    c. supporting schedule.
    d. statement of cash flows.

6. A manager analyzing her menu using the food cost percentage approach needs to know each menu item's food cost percentage and each item's
    a. fixed cost.
    b. popularity.
    c. selling price.
    d. contribution margin.

7. Which menu analysis system utilizes an algebraic equation rather than a matrix to identify profitable menu items?
   a. Food cost percentage
   b. Menu engineering
   c. Goal value analysis
   d. Contribution margin

8. Last week, a manager's operation sold 4,250 menu items, generated $82,000 in sales and achieved a 28 percent food cost. What was the manager's average contribution margin per item sold last week?
   a. $3.40
   b. $4.40
   c. $5.40
   d. $6.40

9. In the menu engineering approach to assessing menu profitability, which characteristics define menu items as plow horses?
   a. high contribution margin; low popularity
   b. high contribution margin; high popularity
   c. low contribution margin; low popularity
   d. low contribution margin; high popularity

10. Calculate the goal value for a menu item with the following characteristics: Food cost = 47 percent; Number sold = 325; Selling price = $16.75; Variable cost = 40 percent.
    a. $268.24
    b. $375.07
    c. $426.21
    d. $561.24

11. Which form of menu analysis has a major weakness that results from it favoring high-priced menu items over lower-priced menu items?
    a. goal value
    b. cost/volume/profit
    c. contribution margin
    d. food cost percentage

12. An operation's break-even point in sales is equal to its
    a. Fixed costs ÷ Contribution margin %.
    b. Fixed costs × Contribution margin %.
    c. Contribution margin % ÷ Fixed costs.
    d. Contribution margin % + Fixed costs.

13. A Chinese buffet has monthly fixed costs of $22,500. The buffet's check average is $12.00 and its variable costs are $7.50 per check. How much revenue must the operation achieve each month to break even?
    a. $45,000
    b. $50,000
    c. $55,000
    d. $60,000

14. A gourmet burger and craft beer pub has a check average of $18.00 and has variable costs per cover sold of $6.00. Fixed costs are $58,000 per month. What is the rounded number of covers per month that must be sold to reach the pub's break-even point?
    a. 3,254
    b. 4,833
    c. 5,179
    d. 6,652

15. A restaurant owner has an after-tax profit goal of $45,000. The owner's tax rate is 28 percent. How much pre-tax profit must this owner generate to achieve his after-tax profit goal?
    a. $62,500
    b. $68,000
    c. $73,500
    d. $79,000

16. To calculate a minimum sales point for staying open for an extended period of time, managers must know their operations' food cost percentage, variable cost percentage, and their
    a. occupancy cost percentage for the time period.
    b. rent expense incurred during the time period.
    c. minimum payroll cost needed for the time period.
    d. maximum payroll cost needed for the time period.

17. Once it is established, an annual budget should NOT be modified.
    a. True
    b. False

18. One advantage of budgets is their ability to assist managers in developing menu prices.
    a. True
    b. False

19. One disadvantage of budgets is their failure to identify when an operation will require supplemental cash flows.
    a. True
    b. False

20. Long-range budgets are typically prepared for a period of three to five years.
    a. True
    b. False

21. Achievement budgets address relatively short periods of time in an operation.
    a. True
    b. False

22. Which type of information needed to create a budget would be unavailable in a soon-to-be-opened foodservice operation?
    a. goals
    b. monitoring policies
    c. prior-period operating results
    d. assumptions of next period operations

23. A manager has created a revenue budget based on 13 accounting periods of 28 days each. The manager has budgeted for revenue of $1,000,000 for the year. How much revenue must the manager generate in each period to achieve her annual revenue budget?
    a. $35,714
    b. $56,401
    c. $76,923
    d. $83,333

24. A manager's operation achieved a 34 percent food cost on sales of $900,000. For next year, the manager anticipates a 5 percent increase in the prices he will pay for food. What should the manager estimate his food cost percentage to be next year if his menu prices are not increased?
    a. 33.7%
    b. 34.7%
    c. 35.7%
    d. 36.7%

25. Last year, a manager's operation achieved a 25 percent labor cost on sales of $1,250,000. For next year, the manager anticipates a 6 percent increase in the price she will pay for labor. The manager will also increase her menu prices by 5 percent. What should be this manager's best estimate for next year's labor cost percentage?
    a. 24.2%
    b. 25.2%
    c. 26.2%
    d. 27.2%

26. Which cost area in a manager's expense budget would be most affected by the impact of weather?
   a. food
   b. labor
   c. utilities
   d. equipment rental

27. Budgets should be continually monitored in the three areas of revenue, expense, and
   a. profit.
   b. selling prices.
   c. contribution margins.
   d. labor productivity ratios.

28. A manager's operation has 176 seats. Last month the manager's operation generated $268,400 in sales. What were this manager's sales per seat last month?
   a. $1,057
   b. $1,525
   c. $6,557
   d. $6,925

29. Last year, a restaurant owner achieved sales of $750,000 and his operation consisted of 125 seats. The manager is considering an expansion for next year that will add an additional 25 seats. What should be this owner's best revenue forecast for next year if he adds the additional 25 seats?
   a. $800,000
   b. $825,000
   c. $850,000
   d. $900,000

30. A manager's pizza operation occupies 800 square feet. Last year, the manager achieved sales per square foot of $550. What was the manager's revenue last year?
   a. $140,000
   b. $240,000
   c. $340,000
   d. $440,000

31. Use of the yardstick method is one way managers can analyze expense standards related to their
   a. fixed costs.
   b. portion costs.
   c. variable costs.
   d. occupancy costs.

Chapter Answers to Key Terms & Concepts Review, Discussion Questions, and Quiz Yourself

Key Terms & Concepts Review

1. g	6. c	11. h	16. d
2. k	7. r	12. j	17. n
3. o	8. e	13. p	18. m
4. a	9. b	14. i	
5. q	10. l	15. f	

Discussion Questions

1. List and explain the three areas of analysis that can assist a manager in planning for profit.
   - Menu analysis: Menu analysis is more than just numbers; it involves marketing, sociology, psychology, and emotions. Guests respond to menu copy, the description of the menu items, and the placement of items on the menu, their menu price, and their current popularity. The ability to analyze a menu for profitability is essential if managers are to achieve their operations' financial goals.
   - Cost/volume/profit (CVP) analysis: CVP (break-even) analysis helps managers predict the sales dollars and volume required to achieve desired profit (or break-even) based on the operation's known costs. When managers can complete a CVP analysis they are in a better position to assess their fixed costs, variable costs, and the marketing and sales efforts required to achieve the minimum levels of revenue needed for their businesses to break-even or make a profit.
   - Budget: Formal budgets will detail the operational direction of units you will manage and your expected financial results. A budget is also commonly known as a "plan" because a formal budget allows managers to plan for future financial events.

2. List and briefly describe the six different operational variables that can be utilized when conducting a menu analysis.
   - Food cost percentage: the proportion of a menu item's selling price that is needed to buy the ingredients required to make the item.
   - Popularity: the frequency at which a menu item sells relative to other menu items.
   - Contribution margin: the amount of money remaining after a menu item's product cost has been subtracted from its selling price.
   - Selling price: The price at which a menu item is sold.
   - Variable expenses: Those expenses of a business that increase or decrease in proportion to the revenue achieved by the business. Examples include the cost of food servers and food costs.

- Fixed expenses: Those expenses of a business that do not increase or decrease in proportion to the revenue achieved by the business. Examples include mortgage payments for buildings, costs of insurance policies, and the expense of required operating permits.

3. Explain the importance to foodservice managers of the "minimum sales point" concept.
   - Most restaurants are not operated 24 hours a day and seven days a week. While some QSRs do operate on such a calendar, in most cases managers must make decisions about the best times to open and close their foodservice operations.

   - The minimum sales point concept is useful because it allows managers to know how much sales volume must be achieved during a particular time in order to justify keeping their business open. When calculating the Minimum Sales Point managers assess three areas:
     1. Food cost %
     2. Minimum payroll cost needed for the time.
     3. Variable cost %
   - A careful assessment of these three areas helps managers know their optimum operating hours, thus allowing them to be open only during times when it makes good sense financially for them to do so.

4. Identify and describe the three main types of foodservice budgets.
   - Long-range budget: Typically prepared for a period of three to five years. It provides a long-term view about where the operation should be going from a financial perspective and can identify areas in which significant expenditures will be required.
   - Annual budget: Typically prepared for a one-year period or, in some cases, one season. These budgets are common because most foodservice operations want to report their operating results at least once per calendar year.
   - Achievement budget: An achievement budget is always shorter range than an annual budget. Achievement budgets typically address a month or a week. These very short-term budgets provide current operating information and thus can assist managers in making current operational decisions.

5. Explain the importance of monitoring each of the three main areas addressed in an operating budget.
   - The three main areas addressed in operating budget are:
     1. Revenue
     2. Expense
     3. Profits
   - Revenue: If revenue falls below its projected levels, the impact on profit can be substantial. If revenue consistently exceeds projections, the overall budget must be modified or the variable expenses associated with these increased sales will soon exceed budgeted amounts.

- Expense: Costs that are too high or too low may be a cause of concern. To help make an expense assessment quickly, some operators elect to utilize the yardstick method of calculating expense standards so determinations can be made as to whether variations in expenses are due only to changes in sales volume or are due to other, undesirable reasons, such as waste or theft.
- Profit: Budgeted profits must be realized if an operation is to provide adequate returns for its owners' and investors' risks. A primary goal of management is to generate the profits necessary for the successful continuation of a business and budgeting for these profits is a fundamental step in the process.

Quiz Yourself

1. b.	9. a.	17. b.	25. b.
2. c.	10. b.	18. a.	26. c.
3. a.	11. c.	19. b.	27. a.
4. a.	12. a.	20. a.	28. b.
5. b.	13. d.	21. a.	29. d.
6. b.	14. b.	22. c.	30. d.
7. c.	15. a.	23. c.	31. c.
8. c.	16. c.	24. c.	

Chapter 11

Maintaining and Improving the Revenue Control System

Learning Outcomes

At the conclusion of this chapter, you will be able to:

- Identify internal and external threats to revenue.

  Most foodservice employees are honest, but some are not. As a result, managers must learn how to protect their revenue from those few employees and even vendors who may attempt to steal the income their facilities have earned. Knowing how to identify these potential internal threats to revenue is crucial.

  In addition to internal threats, there are externals threats, primarily initiated by an operation's customers, which must be guarded against. When managers can do that, they help protect the income and profits their operations generate.

- Create effective countermeasures to combat internal and external theft.

  While it is important to be able to identify internal and external threats to revenue security, it even more important that managers can implement policies and procedures that prevent these threats from creating operational losses of money and other assets.

  When managers know how to create and implement effective countermeasures to combat internal and external theft they minimize the opportunity for unnecessary losses of income in their businesses.

- Establish and monitor a complete and effective revenue security system.

  A complete revenue protection system ensures an operation's assets such as food and drinks, as well as revenue, are secure.

  Managers must know how to establish and monitor revenue security systems that minimize their operations' chances of asset loss. These systems must be maintained and monitored if they are to operate as they are intended. When managers know how to do this, their operations will experience minimal loss despite the myriad internal and external threats to revenue security they may face.

Study Notes

1. Revenue Security

- Errors in revenue collection can come from simple employee mistakes or, in some cases, outright theft by guests, employees, or others.

- An important part of your job is to devise revenue security systems that protect your operation's income, whether you receive it in the form of cash, checks, credit or debit card receipts, coupons, meal cards, or any other method of guest payment.

- In its simplest form, revenue control and security is a matter of matching products sold with funds received.

- An effective revenue security system ensures that the following five formulas reflect what really happens in your foodservice operation:

  1. Documented product requests = Product issues
  2. Product issues (by the kitchen or bar) = Guest charges
  3. Total charges = Sales receipts
  4. Sales receipts = Sales (bank) deposits
  5. Sales deposits = Funds available to pay *legitimate* expenses (called accounts payable)

- The potential for guest or employee theft or fraud exists in all of these five areas.

- Revenue security problems can exist in either of the following areas:

  1. External threats to revenue security
  2. Internal threats to revenue security

2. External Threats to Revenue Security

- A guest is said to have **walked**, or **skipped** a check when he or she has consumed a product but has left the foodservice operation without paying the bill.

- As a manager, you can use a variety of strategies to help reduce the chances that guests will walk their bills. These include:

    1. If guests order and consume their food prior to your receiving payment, instruct servers to present the bill for the food promptly when the guests have finished.

    2. If your facility has a cashier in a central location in the dining area, have that cashier available and visible at all times.

    3. If your facility operates in such a manner that each server collects for his or her own guest's charges, instruct the servers to return to the table promptly after presenting the guest's bill to secure a form of payment.

    4. Train employees to be observant of exit doors near restrooms or other areas of the facility that may provide an unscrupulous guest the opportunity to exit the dining area without being easily seen.

    5. If an employee sees a guest leave without paying the bill, you or another manager should be notified immediately.

    6. Upon approaching a guest who has left without paying the bill, a manager should ask if the guest has inadvertently "forgotten" to pay. In most cases, the guest will then pay the bill.

    7. Should a guest still refuse to pay or flee the scene, a manager should note the following on an incident report:
        a. Number of guests involved
        b. Amount of the bill
        c. Physical description of the guest(s)
        d. Vehicle description/license plate number if the guests flee in a car
        e. Time and date of the incident
        f. Name of the server(s) who served the guest

    8. If the guest is successful in fleeing the scene, the police should be notified. In no case should your staff members or managers be instructed to attempt to physically detain the guest.

- A **quick-change artist** is a guest who, having practiced the routine many times, attempts to confuse a cashier to receive more money in change than they are entitled to.

- Another form of external theft that you must guard against is that of a guest using counterfeit money.

- **Counterfeit money** is an imitation of valid currency intended to be passed off fraudulently as real money. Counterfeit money used by guests will not be honored as legal currency by banks.

- Fraudulent payment attempts can include the use of invalid or falsified credit or debit cards.

- A **credit card** is simply a system by which banks loan money to consumers as the consumer makes purchases.

- **Travel and entertainment (T&E) cards** are a payment system by which the card issuer collects full payment from the card users on a monthly basis.

- A **debit card** is an extremely popular form of guest payment. In this system, the funds needed to cover the user's purchase are automatically transferred from the user's bank account to the entity issuing the debit card.

- If restaurant managers are to ensure that they collect all of the money they are due from payment card companies, they must effectively manage the **interface** (electronic connection) between the various payment card issuers and their restaurant.

- **Merchant service provider (MSP)** plays an important role as the restaurant's coordinator/manager of payment card acceptance and funds collection.

- A restaurant accepting payment cards does not actually "receive" immediate cash from its card sales but, rather, it will be credited via **electronic funds transfer (EFT)** the money it is due after all fees have been paid.

- As a manager, you can use a variety of strategies to help reduce the incident of fraudulent payment card use:

    1. Confirm that the name on the card is the same as that of the individual presenting the card for payment. Drivers' licenses or other acceptable forms of identification can be used.
    2. Examine the card for any obvious signs of alteration.
    3. Confirm that the card is indeed valid, that is, that the card has not expired or is not yet in effect.
    4. Compare the signature on the back of the card with the one produced by the guest paying with the card.
    5. Have the employee processing the charge initial the credit card receipt.
    6. Keep credit card charges that have not yet been processed in a secure place
    7. Do not issue cash in exchange for credit card charges.
    8. Do not write in tip amounts for guests.
    9. Tally credit card charges on a daily basis.
    10. Ensure that only managers approve all cardholder challenges or requests for charge card payment reversals.

3. Internal Threats to Revenue Security

- Most foodservice employees are honest, but some are not.

- Cash is the most readily usable asset in a foodservice operation, and it is a major target for dishonest employees.

- Service personnel can use a variety of techniques to cheat an operation of a small amount of cash at one time.

- One of the most common server theft techniques involves the omission of recording the guest's order. In this situation, the server does not record the sale in the operation's POS, but charges the guest and keeps the revenue from the sale.

- Complete revenue control is a matter of developing the checks and balances necessary to ensure that the value of products sold and the amount of revenue received equal each other.

- Food operations should require a written **guest check** recording each sale. A guest check is simply a written record of what the guest purchased and how much the guest was charged for the item(s).

- The use of paper or electronic guest checks is standard in the hospitality industry today because guest checks also serve as the way employees take guest orders and communicate the orders to those employees responsible for filling them.

- A rule when using guest checks is that no food or beverage should be issued to a server unless the server first records the sale on a guest check.

- Modern point-of-sale (POS) systems assign unique electronic numbers to each guest check they create.

- Paper guest checks should be recorded by number and then safely stored or destroyed after use, as management policy dictates.

- Another method of service personnel fraud is one in which the server gives the proper guest check to the guest, collects payment, and destroys the guest check but keeps the money.

- For this reason, many operators implement a **precheck/postcheck system** for guest checks.

- A **user workstation** is a computer terminal that records items ordered and then displays the order in the production area. In some systems, the order may even be printed in the production area.

- Handheld and wireless at-the-table order entry devices now allow servers (and guests in some cases) to enter prechecked orders directly into an operation's POS system.

- Regardless of how the prechecked guest check is created, kitchen and bar personnel are, in this system, prohibited from issuing any products to the server without a uniquely numbered, prechecked guest check.

- When the guest is ready to leave, the cashier retrieves the prechecked guest check and prepares a postcheck bill for the guest to pay.

- The postcheck total includes the charges for all of the prechecked items ordered by the guest plus any service charges and taxes due.

- The guest then pays the bill.

- In a precheck/postcheck system, products ordered by the guest, prechecked by the server, and issued by the kitchen or bar should match the items and money collected by the cashier.

- There can be reasons why initial prechecked sales totals do not match the amount of money collected by the cashier. Many times, guests place orders and then change their minds, adding or subtracting from their original orders. In other cases, an ordered item may be returned by a guest and, depending on the reason for the item's return, the guest may not be charged for it.

- Another method of employee theft involves failing to finalize a sale recorded on the precheck and pocketing the money. To prevent such theft, management must have systems in place to identify open checks during and after each server's work shift.

- **Open checks** are those that have been used to authorize product issues from the kitchen or bar but that have not been collected for (closed) and thus have not been added to the operation's sales total.

- The totals of guest checks rung on the POS during a predetermined period are electronically tallied, so management can compare the sales recorded by the POS with the money actually contained in the cash drawer. Cashiers rarely steal large sums directly from the cash drawer because such theft is easily detected.

- Only managers should compare the sales recorded by the cash register with the money actually contained in the cash register. If it contains less than sales recorded, it is said to be **short;** if it contains more than sales recorded, it is said to be **over**.

- Consistent cash shortages may be an indication of employee theft or carelessness.

- Cash overages, too, may be the result of sophisticated theft by the cashier.

- Some companies protect themselves from employee dishonesty by bonding their employees.

- **Bonding** involves management purchasing an insurance policy against the possibility that an employee(s) will steal.

- If an employee has been bonded and an operation can determine that he or she was indeed involved in the theft of a specific amount of money, the operation will be reimbursed for the loss by the bonding company.

- Even good revenue control systems present the opportunity for theft if management is not vigilant or if two or more employees conspire to defraud the operation (**collusion**).

4. Developing the Revenue Security System

- An effective revenue security system will help you accomplish the following important tasks:

  - Verification of product issues
  - Verification of guest charges
  - Verification of sales receipts
  - Verification of sales deposits
  - Verification of accounts payable

- In an ideal world, a product would be sold, its sale recorded, its selling price collected, the funds deposited in the foodservice operation's bank account, and the cost of providing the product would be paid for, all in a single step. Rapid advances in the area of computers and "smart" cards are making this more of a reality for more foodservice operators each day.

- The five-step process of revenue security results in a system that ensures:

  > Product issues = Guest charges = Sales receipts = Sales deposits = Funds available for accounts payable

- The key to verification of product issues in the revenue security system is to follow one basic rule: *No product should be issued from the kitchen or bar unless a permanent record of the issue is made.*

$$\boxed{\text{Documented product requests} = \text{Product issues}}$$

- When the production staff is required to distribute products only in response to a documented request, it is critical that those documented requests result in charges to the guest. *Product issues must equal guest charges.*

- Each guest check must be accounted for, and employees must know that they will be held responsible for each check they are issued.

$$\boxed{\text{Product issues} = \text{Guest charges}}$$

- Sales receipts refer to actual revenue received by the cashier or other designated personnel, in payment for products served. *Both the cashier and a member of management must verify sales receipts.*

$$\boxed{\text{Total charges} = \text{Sales receipts}}$$

- Sales receipts refer to all forms of revenue, such as cash, checks (if accepted), and bank (credit or debit) cards as well as prepaid cards.

- In general, there are five basic payment arrangements in use in typical foodservice operations:

   1. Guest pays cashier.
   2. Guest pays at the table.
   3. Guest pays service personnel, who pay cashier.
   4. Guest pays service personnel, who have already paid cashier.
   5. Guest is direct billed.

- In some cases, variations on the five payment systems presented can be put in place, such as the drink ticket, or coupon sold or issued in hotel reception areas for use at cocktail receptions.

- It is strongly recommended that only management make the actual bank deposit of daily sales revenue.

- A cashier or other clerical assistant may complete the deposit slip, but management alone should bear the responsibility for monitoring the actual deposit of sales. This concept can be summarized as follows: *Management must personally verify all bank deposits.* This involves the actual verification of the contents of the deposit and the process of matching bank deposits with actual sales.

- **Embezzlement** is the term used to describe employee theft where the embezzler takes company funds he or she was entrusted to keep and diverts them to personal use.

- Falsification of bank deposits is a common method of embezzlement. To prevent this activity, you should take the following steps to protect your deposits:

  1. Make bank deposits of cash and checks daily if possible.
  2. Ensure that the person preparing the deposit is not the one making the deposit-unless you or the manager do both tasks. Also, ensure that the individual making the daily deposit is bonded.
  3. Establish written policies for completing **bank reconciliations**, the regularly scheduled comparison of the business's deposit records with the bank's acceptance records. Payment card funds transfers to a business's bank account should be reconciled each time they occur. Increasingly, cash and payment card reconciliations can be accomplished on a daily basis via the use of online banking features.
  4. Review and approve written bank statement reconciliations at least once each month.
  5. Change combinations on safes periodically and share the combinations with the fewest employees possible.
  6. Require that all cash-handling employees take regular and uninterrupted vacations on a regular basis so that another employee can assume and uncover any improper practices.
  7. Employ an outside auditor to examine the accuracy of deposits on an annual basis.

- If verification of sales deposits is done correctly and no embezzlement is occurring, the following formula should hold true:

Sales receipts = Sales deposits

- **Accounts payable** refers to the legitimate amount owed to a vendor for the purchase of products or services.

- The basic principle to be followed when verifying accounts payable is: *The individual authorizing the purchase should verify the legitimacy of the vendor's invoice before it is paid.*

- In a revenue system that is working properly, the following formula should be in effect:

Sales deposits = Funds available for accounts payable

- In some situations, guests are not billed immediately upon finishing their meal, beverages, or reception, but are **direct billed** for their charges. When this is the case, creditworthy guests are sent a bill for the value of the products they have consumed after their event is over. When this form of billing is employed, it is important that the invoice sent accurately reflects all guest charges.

- **Accounts receivable** is the term used to refer to guest charges that have been billed to the guest but not yet collected.

- Too high an accounts receivable amount should be avoided because the foodservice operation has paid for the products consumed by the guest and the labor to serve the products but has not yet collected from the guests for these.

- Another special pricing situation is the reduced-price coupon. Coupons are popular in the hospitality industry and can take a variety of forms, such as 50 percent off a specific purchase, "buy-one-get-one-free" (BOGO) promotions, or a program whereby a guest who buys a predetermined number of items or meals gets the next one free.

- In all of these cases, coupons should be treated as its cash equivalent because, from a revenue control perspective, these coupons are equivalent to cash.

5. The Complete Revenue Security System

- The five summary principles of a revenue security system are that:

  1. No product shall be issued from the kitchen or bar unless a permanent record of the issue is made.
  2. Product issues must equal guest charges.
  3. Both the cashier and a supervisor must verify sales receipts.
  4. Management must personally verify all bank deposits.
  5. Management or the individual authorizing the purchase should verify the legitimacy of the vendor's invoice before it is paid.

- It is possible to develop and maintain a completely manual revenue control system. However, when properly selected and understood, technology-enhanced systems can be a powerful ally in the cost control/revenue security system.

6. Technology Tools

- Protecting sales revenue from external and internal threats of theft requires diligence and attention to detail. Software and specialized hardware now on the market that can help in this area includes those that:

  1. Maintain daily cash balances from all sources, including those of multiunit and international operations.
  2. Reconcile inventory reductions with product issues from kitchen.
  3. Reconcile product issues from kitchen with guest check totals.
  4. Reconcile guest check totals with revenue totals.
  5. Create over and short computations by server, shift, and day.
  6. Balance daily bank deposits with daily sales revenue and identify variances.
  7. Maintain database of returned checks.
  8. Maintain accounts receivable records.
  9. Maintain accounts payable records.
  10. Maintain records related to the sale and redemption of gift cards.
  11. Interface back office accounting systems with data compiled by the operation's POS system.
  12. Interface budgeting software with revenue generation software.
  13. Create income statements, statements of cash flows, and balance sheets.

- It is important to note that interfacing (electronically connecting) the various software programs an operation chooses to use is very helpful.

Key Terms & Concepts Review

Match the key terms with their correct definitions.

1. Walk, or skip (the bill) _____
   a. Cards in a payment system by which the card issuer collects full payment from the card users on a monthly basis. These card companies do not typically assess their users' interest charges.

2. Quick-change artist _____
   b. The theft of credit card information used in an otherwise legitimate transaction.

3. Counterfeit money _____
   c. Electronic connection for the purpose of sharing data.

4. Credit cards _____
   d. Provides for the electronic payment and collection of money and information; it is a safe, secure, efficient, and less expensive than paper check payments and collections.

5. Travel and entertainment (T&E) cards _____
   e. Term used when the total amount of money in a cash drawer is less than the total amount of money that should be there based on sales receipts.

6. Debit cards _____
   f. A term used to describe a customer who has consumed a product, but leaves the foodservice operation without paying the bill.

7. Interface _____
   g. The term used to describe theft of a type where the money, although legally possessed by the embezzler, is diverted to the embezzler by his or her fraudulent action.

8. Merchant service provider (MSP) _____
   h. Term used when the total amount of money in a cash drawer is more than the total amount of money that should be there based on sales receipts.

9. Electronic funds transfer (EFT) _____
   i. The term used to refer to guest charges that have been billed to guests but not yet collected from them.

237

10. Credit card skimming	_____	j.	A guest check that has been used to authorize product issues from the kitchen or bar in an operation, but that has not been collected for (closed) and thus the amount of the open check has not been added to the operation's sales total.
11. Guest check	_____	k.	A guest who, having practiced the routine many times, attempts to confuse the cashier so that the cashier, in his or her confusion, will give the guest too much change.
12. Precheck/postcheck system	_____	l.	The legitimate amount owed to vendors for products received or services rendered.
13. User workstation	_____	m.	A written record of what was purchased by the guest and how much the guest was charged for the item(s).
14. Open check	_____	n.	A comparison of a business's deposit and disbursements records with its bank's acceptance and disbursement records.
15. Short	_____	o.	Purchasing an insurance policy to protect the operation in case of employee theft.
16. Over	_____	p.	Cards in a payment system by which banks loan money to consumers as the consumer makes purchases. The loans typically carry interest.
17. Bonding	_____	q.	A computer terminal used only to ring up (record) food and beverage orders.
18. Collusion	_____	r.	Guests are not billed immediately upon consuming products and services, but are sent a bill for the value of the products and services after their visit or event is over.

19. Embezzlement	_____	s.	A restaurant's coordinator/manager of payment card acceptance and funds collection, and it provides the electronic connection between payment card issuers and their merchants.
20. Bank reconciliation	_____	t.	An imitation of currency intended to be passed off fraudulently as real money.
21. Accounts payable	_____	u.	The server records the order (prechecks) on a guest check when the order is given to him or her by the guest. The products ordered by the guest, prechecked by the server, and issued by the kitchen or bar, should match the items and money collected by the cashier (postcheck).
22. Direct billed	_____	v.	Cards in a payment system by which the funds needed to cover the user's purchase are automatically transferred from the user's bank account to the entity issuing the debit card.
23. Accounts receivable	_____	w.	Secret cooperation between two or more individuals that is intended to defraud an operation.

Discussion Questions

1. List and explain five formulas that can help a manager maintain an effective revenue security system.

   _____
   _____
   _____
   _____

2. List five of the eight steps that help to reduce guest walks, or skips.

   _____
   _____
   _____
   _____

3. Describe how a precheck/postcheck system helps managers minimize theft by front-of-house and back-of-house employees.

   _____
   _____
   _____
   _____

4. List five tasks a manager must consider when developing a total revenue security system.

   _____
   _____
   _____
   _____

5. Explain why managers should avoid excessive levels of accounts receivables.

   _____
   _____
   _____
   _____

Quiz Yourself

Choose the letter of the best answer to the questions listed below.

1. In which type of restaurant are guests least likely to skip a bill?
   a. QSR
   b. buffet
   c. steak house
   d. family style

2. If guests order and consume menu items prior to paying for them, their bills should be presented to them promptly after they
   a. order.
   b. have finished.
   c. receive their items.
   d. ask for their check.

3. Who must be well-trained to avoid being victimized by quick-change artists?
   a. cooks
   b. servers
   c. cashiers
   d. managers

4. Which type of payment card requires the card holder to pay his or her balance in full each month?
   a. bank
   b. debit
   c. credit
   d. travel and entertainment

5. Merchant service providers coordinate a restaurant's
   a. cashier training programs.
   b. guest check numbering system.
   c. monitoring of cash register overs and shorts.
   d. payment card acceptance and funds collection.

6. Who would be responsible for fraud involving credit card skimming at a restaurant?
   a. MSP
   b. guests
   c. vendors
   d. employees

7. Who is most often responsible for entering precheck data in a restaurant using a precheck/postcheck system?
   a. cooks
   b. guests
   c. servers
   d. managers

Use the information below to answer Questions 8 through 10.

Tim is the manager at a restaurant. The following are the amounts in his cashier's drawer when counted and the amounts of guest charges recorded in his POS system.

Day	Amount in Cashiers' Drawers	Guest Charges Per POS	Over/(Short)
Monday	$10,568.54	$10,540.20	
Tuesday	$11,698.82	$11,708.24	
Wednesday	$13,216.35	$13,220.97	
Thursday	$9,698.67	$9,705.21	
Friday	$14,987.63	$14,982.52	
Saturday	$15,468.15	$15,470.25	
Sunday	$11,568.74	$11,568.76	
Total	$87,206.90	$87,196.15	

8. What were Tim's total overs/shorts for the week?
   a. $15.25 over
   b. $10.75 short
   c. $10.75 over
   d. $15.25 short

9. What was the average amount per day of Tim's total overs/shorts for the week?
   a. $0.54
   b. $1.54
   c. $15.40
   d. $154.00

10. On what day did Tim's operation experience its largest over/short amount?
    a. Monday
    b. Thursday
    c. Friday
    d. Saturday

11. Who will be reimbursed if a restaurant has bonded an employee who is later found to have defrauded the operation?
    a. the operation's bank
    b. the operation's owner
    c. the operation's guests
    d. the operation's employees

12. No product should be issued from the kitchen or bar unless a
    a. guest orders the product.
    b. manager authorizes the product's issue.
    c. permanent record of the issue is made.
    d. form of guest payment is secured prior to product issue.

13. What is the first concept managers must ensure is in place when designing an effective revenue control system?
    a. Total charges = Sales receipts
    b. Sales receipts = Sales deposits
    c. Documented product requests = Products issued
    d. Sales deposits = Funds available for accounts payable

14. Both the cashier and a member of management must verify
    a. sales receipts.
    b. bank deposits.
    c. product issues.
    d. accounts receivable.

15. Which is the most likely form of employee embezzlement at a bar?
    a. overpouring drinks
    b. falsification of POS records
    c. falsification of bank deposits
    d. over-payment of vendor invoices

16. Bank reconciliations performed by managers help ensure the verification of
    a. sales receipts.
    b. sales deposits.
    c. product issues.
    d. accounts payable.

17. Managers should undertake a bank reconciliation at least once per
    a. day.
    b. week.
    c. month.
    d. year.

18. A meat vendor submits an invoice for payment. Verification of the legitimacy of the invoice prior to its payment should be done by the individual who
    a. stored the meat.
    b. issued the meat.
    c. ordered the meat.
    d. received the meat.

19. Accounts receivable are amounts that have been billed to
    a. and collected from an operation's guests.
    b. an operation by its vendors and have been paid.
    c. but not yet collected from, an operation's guests.
    d. an operation by its vendors but have not yet been paid.

20. Permanent records of product issuing are just one of several ways products can be legitimately dispensed from a kitchen or bar.
    a. True
    b. False

21. In a foodservice operation, product issues should equal guest charges.
    a. True
    b. False

22. Only cashiers should verify the sales receipts in their cash drawers.
    a. True
    b. False

23. Bank deposits may be verified by either managers or cashiers.
    a. True
    b. False

24. The individual accepting delivery of an ordered product should verify the legitimacy of the vendor's invoice for the product before the invoice is paid.
    a. True
    b. False

Chapter Answers to Key Terms & Concepts Review, Discussion Questions, and Quiz Yourself

Key Terms & Concepts Review

1. f	6. v	11. m	16. h	21. l
2. k	7. c	12. u	17. o	22. r
3. t	8. s	13. q	18. w	23. i
4. p	9. d	14. j	19. g	
5. a	10. b	15. e	20. n	

Discussion Questions

1. List and explain five formulas that can help a manager maintain an effective revenue security system.
   - Documented product requests = Product issues. No product should be issued from the kitchen or bar unless a permanent record of the issue is made.
   - Product issues = Guest charges. Product issues must equal guest charges.
   - Total charges = Sales receipts. Both the cashier and a member of management must verify sales receipts.
   - Sales receipts = Sales (bank) deposits. Management must personally verify all bank deposits.
   - Sales deposits = Accounts payable for legitimate expenses. The authorized purchaser must verify the legitimacy of accounts payable to be paid out of sales deposits.

2. List five of the eight steps that help to reduce guest walks, or skips.
   - If the custom of a restaurant is that guests order and consume their goods prior to your receiving payment, instruct servers to present the bill for the food promptly when the guests have finished.
   - If a facility has a cashier in a central location in the dining area, have that cashier available and visible at all times.
   - If a facility operates in such a manner that each server collects for his or her own guest's charges, instruct the servers to return to the table promptly after presenting the guest's bill to secure a form of payment.
   - Train employees to be observant of exit doors near restrooms or other areas of the facility that may provide an unscrupulous guest the opportunity to exit the dining area without being easily seen.
   - If an employee sees a guest leave without paying the bill, management should be notified immediately.

- Upon approaching a guest who has left without paying the bill, the manager should ask if the guest has inadvertently "forgotten" to pay. In most cases, the guest will then pay the bill.
- If a guest still refuses to pay or flees the scene, the manager should note the following on an incident report:
  - Number of guests involved
  - Amount of the bill
  - Physical description of the guest(s)
  - Vehicle description if the guests flee in a car, as well as the license plate number if possible
  - Time and date of the incident
  - Name of the server(s) who actually served the guest
- If the guest is successful in fleeing the scene, the police should be notified. In no case should your staff member or managers be instructed to attempt to physically detain the guest.

3. Describe how a precheck/postcheck system helps managers minimize theft by front-of-house and back-of-house employees.

- In a precheck/postcheck system, the dining room server writes guest orders on a piece of paper for subsequent entry into a POS terminal. The terminal records the items ordered and then may display the order in the production area. No item is to be issued by the kitchen unless there is a document recording the server's request.
- A precheck/postcheck system helps minimize server theft in the front-of-the-house because no server can secure items from the kitchen or bar without a record being made of them doing so. This helps minimize the chances that servers will deliver items to guests, collect the money for those items, but not report the income.
- A precheck/postcheck system helps minimize back-of-house theft because a record is made of each item served. This helps prevent kitchen employees from stealing products, or from giving products to servers for an unscrupulous sale in which the front-of-house and back-of-house employees collude to steal money from the operation.

4. List five tasks a manager must consider when developing a total revenue security system.
- Verification of product issues
- Verification of guest charges
- Verification of sales receipts
- Verification of sales deposits
- Verification of accounts payable

5. Explain why managers should avoid excessive levels of accounts receivables.
- Accounts receivable is the total amount of guest charges that have been billed to guests but not yet collected.

- An accounts receivable total that is excessively high should be avoided because the foodservice operation has paid for the products consumed by guests and the labor required to prepare and serve the products but has not yet collected from the guests for these costs. When accounts receivable totals are too high, it means the operation has expended significant amounts of money and not yet been repaid for those expenses. This could leave an operation short of operating cash.
- In addition, collecting money after a guest has left an operation can be more difficult as time passes. Expenses will be incurred in billing and follow-up to try to secure payment, and inevitably, some guests will not pay. When that happens, these costs must be absorbed by the operation.
- An appropriate accounts receivable level must be established by management, and it should not be excessive for the size of the operation.

Quiz Yourself

1. a.	7. c.	13. c.	19. c.
2. b.	8. c.	14. a.	20. b.
3. c.	9. b.	15. b.	21. a.
4. d.	10. a.	16. b.	22. b.
5. d.	11. b.	17. c.	23. b.
6. d.	12. c.	18. c.	24. b.

CPSIA information can be obtained at www.ICGtesting.com
Printed in the USA
BVOW05n1048161015

422506BV00001B/1/P